publishing a blog
with Blogger
second edition

Visual QuickProject Guide

by Elizabeth Castro

Peachpit
Press

Visual QuickProject Guide
Publishing a Blog with Blogger, Second Edition
Elizabeth Castro

Peachpit Press
1249 Eighth Street
Berkeley, CA 94710
510/524-2178
510/524-2221 (fax)
Find us on the Web at: www.peachpit.com
To report errors, please send a note to errata@peachpit.com

Peachpit Press is a division of Pearson Education
Copyright © 2010 by Elizabeth Castro
Cover design: Peachpit Press, Aren Howell
Cover photo credit: Photodisc
Interior design and photographs: Elizabeth Castro

Notice of Liability
The information in this book is distributed on an "As Is" basis, without warranty. While every precaution has been taken in the preparation of the book, neither the author nor Peachpit Press shall have any liability to any person or entity with respect to any loss or damage caused or alleged to be caused directly or indirectly by the instructions contained in this book or by the computer software and hardware products described in it.

Trademarks
Visual QuickProject Guide is a registered trademark of Peachpit Press, a division of Pearson Education. All other trademarks are the property of their respective owners.
Throughout this book, trademarks are used. Rather than put a trademark symbol with every occurrence of a trademarked name, we state that we are using the names in an editorial fashion only and to the benefit of the trademark owner with no intention of infringement of the trademark. No such use, or the use of any trade name, is intended to convey endorsement or other affiliation with this book.

ISBN-13: 978-0-321-63752-9
ISBN-10: 0-321-63752-6

9 8 7 6 5 4 3 2 1
Printed and bound in the United States of America

Per a l'Andreu

Special thanks to...

Rick Klau and Brett Wiltshire at Google for their
   invaluable help with Blogger details and patient
   answers to my nitpicky questions;

my dear old friend Nancy Bea Miller, who reminded me
   about blogging just at the perfect moment, inspired me
   with her lovely blog (www.genrecookshop.com), and
   who encourages me by reading and responding to so
   many of my blog posts;

Cliff Colby, my wonderful new editor, and David Van Ness
   at Peachpit Press for their careful editing, sharp eyes,
   and helpful suggestions;

and to Andreu, who continues to make it possible for me
   to write books.

contents

introduction   vii
what you'll do   viii
how this book works   x
the web site   xii
blogger in draft   xiii
useful tools   xiv
getting help   xv
an additional resource   xvi

1. starting your blog   1
start at blogger.com   2
set up an account   3
name your blog   4
choose a template   5
publish your first post   6
the dashboard   8
use the new post editor   9
sign out and in   10
extra bits   11

2. writing your blog   13
add a new post   14
edit a post   16
add a link   18
save a draft   20
publish a draft   21
add formatting   22
add a jump break   24
add labels   26
change the date/time   27
control commenting   28
delete a post   29
extra bits   30

3. adding multimedia   33
upload images   34
place an(other) image   36
move an image   37
wrap text around   38
resize an image   40
remove an image   42
view images on Picasa   43
embed YouTube videos   44
add audio   46
extra bits   48

4. personalizing your blog   51
layout settings   52
page elements   53
reorder page elements   54
add a description   55
add a header image   56
edit Blog Posts area   58
remove a gadget   60
add a gadget   61
add a Link List gadget   62
add Slideshow gadget   64
add Labels gadget   66
change colors   68
change fonts   70
change date display   72
archive daily   73
extra bits   74

5. working with templates   75
pick a new template   76
adjust a new template   78
edit a template   79
add a variable   80
use a new variable   81
back up a template   82
extra bits   83

contents

6. blogging from afar   **85**

set up SMS blogging   86
blog via SMS   87
set up MMS blogging   88
blog via MMS   89
set up email blogging   90
blog via email   91
blog from the toolbar   92
extra bits   94

7. telling others about yourself   **95**

the About Me gadget   96
view your profile   98
edit your profile   99
edit privacy settings   100
edit identity settings   101
add photo to profile   102
add audio to profile   103
add general info   104
add searchable bits   105
search other profiles   106
extra bits   108

8. getting others to contribute   **111**

leave/view comments   112
allow anonymity   114
require humans   115
moderate comments   116
get notified   117
delete comments   118
stop comments   119
hide comments   120
display backlinks   121
create a backlink   122
add a blog author   123
join another's blog   124
share responsibility   126
remove an author   127
restrict access   128
extra bits   129

9. getting the word out   **133**

list your blog   134
email new posts   135
syndicate your blog   136
add subscription links   137
encourage followers   138
follow other blogs   139
share posts   140
let visitors email posts   141
get indexed   142
track your visitors   143
analyze your traffic   146
extra bits   148

10. getting paid to blog   **151**

about AdSense   152
set up AdSense   153
add an AdSense gadget   154
adjust ad placement   155
add inline ads   156
use the AdSense site   157
ad units vs. link units   158
format and colors   159
track ads with channels   160
name your ad   161
place the ad   162
track your earnings   163
other affiliate programs   164
extra bits   165

a. using your own domain   **167**

choose a custom domain   168
tell your registrar   169
extra bits   170

index   **171**

introduction

The Visual QuickProject Guide that you hold in your hands offers a unique way to learn about new technologies. Instead of drowning you in theoretical possibilities and lengthy explanations, this Visual QuickProject Guide uses big, color illustrations coupled with clear, concise step-by-step instructions to show you how to complete one specific project in a matter of hours.

Our project in this book is to create a Web log, or blog, using Google's online Blogger software. A blog is a clever combination of database and web site that lets you focus on writing while a computer program, in this case Blogger, dates and archives your entries and then automatically generates a web site that not only contains what you've written that day but also contains links to all your previous entries. The blog you'll create in this book is a simple, online journal, complete with photographs and links. Because the project covers all the basic techniques, you'll be able to use what you learn to create all sorts of other blogs—perhaps to begin an online newspaper, showcase a frequently updated photography portfolio, or work on a team project using a blog both as a communication tool and also for archiving the team's progress.

Why use Blogger to create your blog? Blogger is one of the most popular online blogging tools, works with any modern browser, and is free, well designed, and easy to use. The Web pages it generates follow current standards for both XHTML and CSS. And it offers beautiful, professionally-designed templates for formatting your blog. In addition, Blogger offers free blog hosting in exchange for a minimal bit of advertising. It's a great choice.

what you'll do

Have Blogger host your blog for free, and/or use your own domain name.

Create a title and a description so that visitors know what your blog is about.

Format the date with just the name of the day, as shown here, or with the complete date and time.

Post individual blog entries, complete with photos, formatting, and links. You'll learn how to blog via your browser, your email program, or even your telephone.

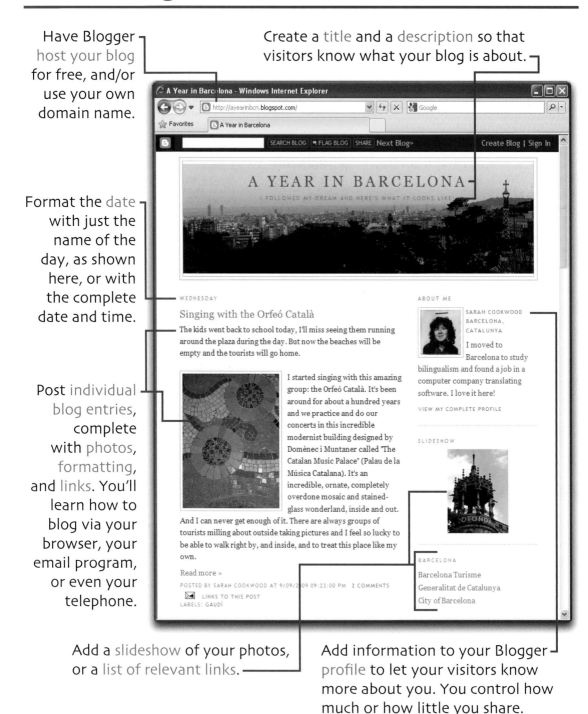

Add a slideshow of your photos, or a list of relevant links.

Add information to your Blogger profile to let your visitors know more about you. You control how much or how little you share.

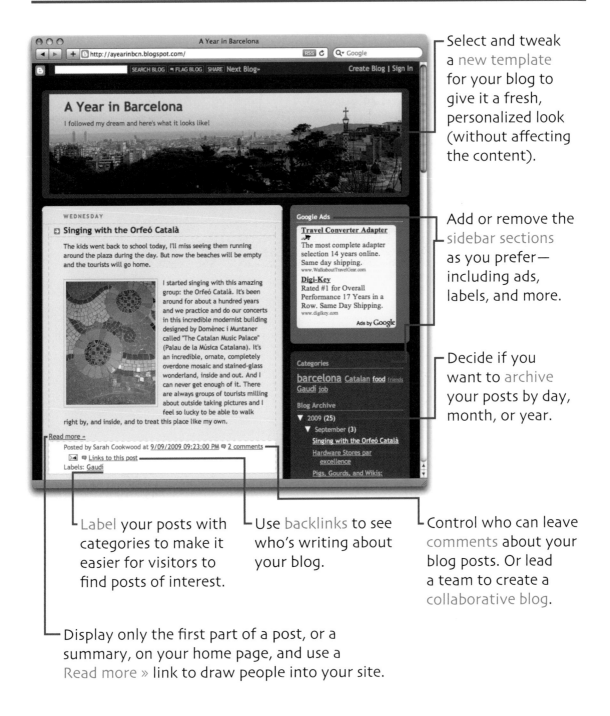

Select and tweak a new template for your blog to give it a fresh, personalized look (without affecting the content).

Add or remove the sidebar sections as you prefer—including ads, labels, and more.

Decide if you want to archive your posts by day, month, or year.

Label your posts with categories to make it easier for visitors to find posts of interest.

Use backlinks to see who's writing about your blog.

Control who can leave comments about your blog posts. Or lead a team to create a collaborative blog.

Display only the first part of a post, or a summary, on your home page, and use a Read more » link to draw people into your site.

how this book works

The title of each section explains what is covered on that page. ⌐

Blogger's pages are named according to the tabs you must click to make them appear. So, to get to the Posting | New Post page, click the Posting tab and then the New Post tab.

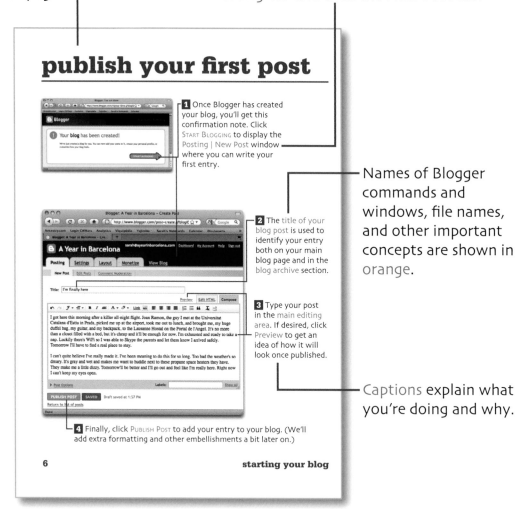

publish your first post

1 Once Blogger has created your blog, you'll get this confirmation note. Click START BLOGGING to display the Posting | New Post window where you can write your first entry.

2 The title of your blog post is used to identify your entry both on your main blog page and in the blog archive section.

Names of Blogger commands and windows, file names, and other important concepts are shown in orange.

3 Type your post in the main editing area. If desired, click Preview to get an idea of how it will look once published.

Captions explain what you're doing and why.

4 Finally, click PUBLISH POST to add your entry to your blog. (We'll add extra formatting and other embellishments a bit later on.)

6   **starting your blog**

The extra bits section at the end of each chapter contains additional tips and tricks that you might like to know—but that aren't absolutely necessary for creating the blog.

The heading for each group of tips matches the section title. (The background colors help distinguish one tip section from the next.)

the dashboard

extra bits

set up an account p. 3
- A Google account gives you access to all of Google's services (Blogger, Gmail, Google Groups, etc.), but you have to sign up for each service individually.

- You can sign up for a Google account with a non-Google email address. In that case, the password that you choose for your Google account does not have to match the one you use to retrieve your email.

- If you don't already have an email account, you can create one with Gmail (http://www.gmail.com). Because Gmail is also part of Google, this will automatically create a Google account which you can then also use to sign in to Blogger (though you'll have to accept Blogger's Terms of Service the first time you create a blog).

- If you already have a Google account and have already signed up for Blogger, you can log in, create a new blog from your Dashboard and then follow the rest of the instructions in this chapter to create your new blog.

- The email address you give will also identify any emails sent from your blog.

name your blog p. 4
- While you can have a blog with the same title as someone else's, the Blog address (URL) you choose must be unique. If you happen to type one that's already in use, you'll get an error and a chance to try another.

choose a template p. 5
- If you don't like any of the given templates, don't fret. You'll learn how to choose a different template (from a wider selection) or modify the template according to your own style in Chapter 5.

publish your first post p. 6
- You don't have to create your first post right away. You can sign out as described on page 10 and then after a rest, start from Chapter 2, where you can add a new post on page 16 .

the dashboard p. 8
- You can have as many blogs as you like. They will all be listed in the Dashboard and be treated independently by Blogger. They are all identified with the Blogger user name that you created on page 3.

Next to the heading there's a page number that shows where you can find the section to which the tips belong.

introduction   **xi**

the web site

You can find the book's companion web site at http://www.elizabethcastro.com/blogvqj/

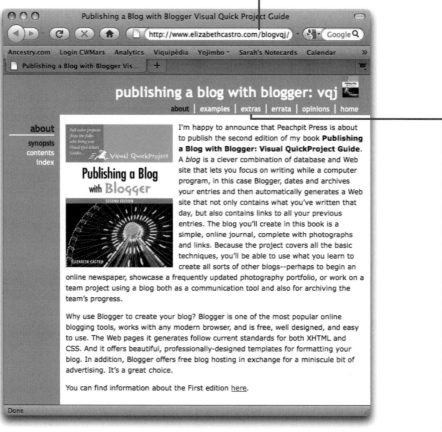

Be sure to visit the extras section, where you'll find a complete list of HTML elements, CSS properties, color codes, errata, and more.

blogger in draft

This book talks about features that are available in the official Blogger. There is also a draft version of Blogger where new features—which may not have all the kinks worked out—are introduced and perfected. You can peek at Blogger in draft to see what's coming, or even use it to write your blog.

1 To open your blog with Blogger in draft, go to http://draft.blogger.com. (Google automatically changes the URL if you're not logged in, so that address is not shown here.)

2 Sign in with your Blogger/ Google account (which you'll create on page 3).

At first glance, Blogger in draft doesn't look that different from the official version, except for the drafting table background.

But as you dig around, you'll notice that there are a number of new and different features, unique to the draft version. Enjoy!

You can also find Blogger news at http://buzz.blogger.com

useful tools

The most important tools for creating a blog are a computer and a browser. It doesn't matter if your computer runs Windows, Unix/Linux, or Macintosh system software. As for browsers, while Blogger's basic functions will work in most browsers, some features are only supported in the most modern of them, like the excellent, fast, and free Mozilla-based Firefox, shown here.

An image editor is useful for retouching and resizing photographs and graphic images for your blog. Many digital cameras and scanners come bundled with some kind of image editor, like Adobe Photoshop Elements, shown here.

getting help

Click Blogger's Help link at the top right of any Blogger page (or point your browser to http://help.blogger.com) to get to Blogger's detailed and useful Help pages.

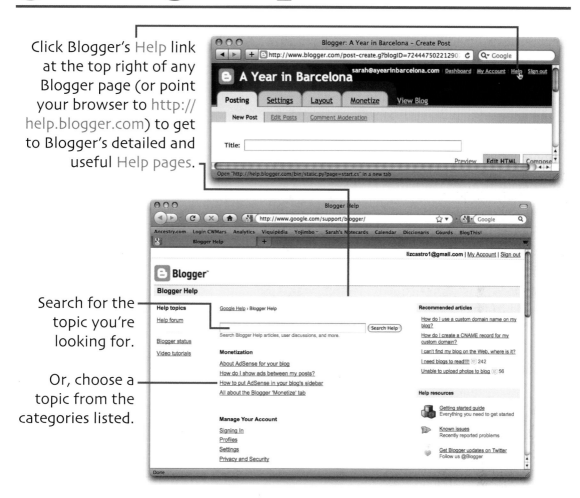

Search for the topic you're looking for.

Or, choose a topic from the categories listed.

Blogger's status page at http://status.blogger.com, lets you know if Blogger itself or its servers are experiencing any problems so at least you know when it's not your fault.

an additional resource

Blogger can generate your blog pages all on its own. However, for formatting your blog (that is, editing Blogger's templates), you may need a more complete resource, like my HTML, XHTML, and CSS, 6th Edition: Visual QuickStart Guide, also published by Peachpit Press. It'll also come in handy if you want to create some non-blog Web pages.

The HTML VQS features clear examples, concise, step-by-step instructions, hundreds of color illustrations, and lots of helpful tips. It covers every aspect of HTML, XHTML, and CSS in detail. It is the number one bestselling guide to HTML.

1. starting your blog

Blogger makes starting your blog an easy three-step process. First, you create an account with Blogger and set some basic preferences for your blog (like its name). Next, you choose a template for your blog's initial design. Finally, you get to the good part: posting your first blog entry.

start at blogger.com

To begin, open your favorite browser and go to Blogger's site: http://www.blogger.com. You should see a window similar to this one. Click CREATE A BLOG to begin.

Since Blogger is owned by Google, if you already have a Google account, you can sign in at the top-right of the screen and then use that account to sign up for Blogger as well.

It doesn't matter if you use a Mac, PC, or Unix/Linux computer. Shown here is the Blogger site on a Mac. On the opposite page you can see Blogger on a PC running Windows.

set up an account

1 Your account with Google/Blogger is what gives you access to your blog. Your existing email address will be your user name. The password you assign yourself here will ensure that only you can go in and create and edit your blogs.

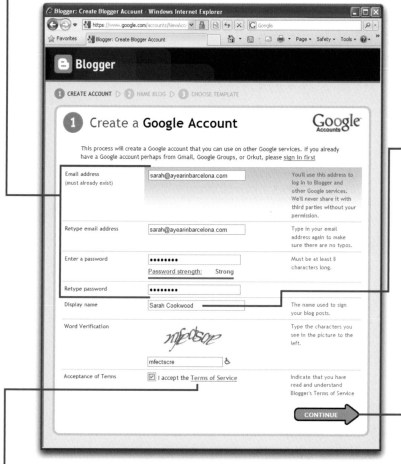

2 The Display Name is the name that is posted at the end of each of your entries in your blog. It's your blog signature.

3 Read Blogger's Terms of Service before you agree to it. Note that Blogger and BlogSpot are two different services. The first is the program that generates the files of your blog; the second is the service that hosts your blog and makes it available to the Web. You can use Blogger with or without BlogSpot.

4 Click Continue.

name your blog

1 The title of your blog is like the title of a book: it must somehow capture the essence of what you're trying to write— and catch your readers' interest at the same time. (This example blog is about living for a year in Barcelona.)

2 Create a simplified version of your title to be used as part of your Blog address (URL). You want it to be easy for your readers both to remember and to type. Only numbers, the letters in the English alphabet, and the dash (-) are permitted (and the dash must not be the first character). Other symbols will produce an error. Capitalized letters are automatically converted to lowercase.

3 Click CONTINUE.

Your blog address must be unique. To be sure someone isn't already using your desired address, click the Check Availability link.

If you get the "Sorry, this blog address is not available" error, you know you have to choose another address.

choose a template

A template determines the formatting that Blogger applies as it converts your posts into the Web pages that make up your blog. For now, you will choose one of Blogger's predefined templates. You'll learn how to choose a different template or edit parts of a template later in the book.

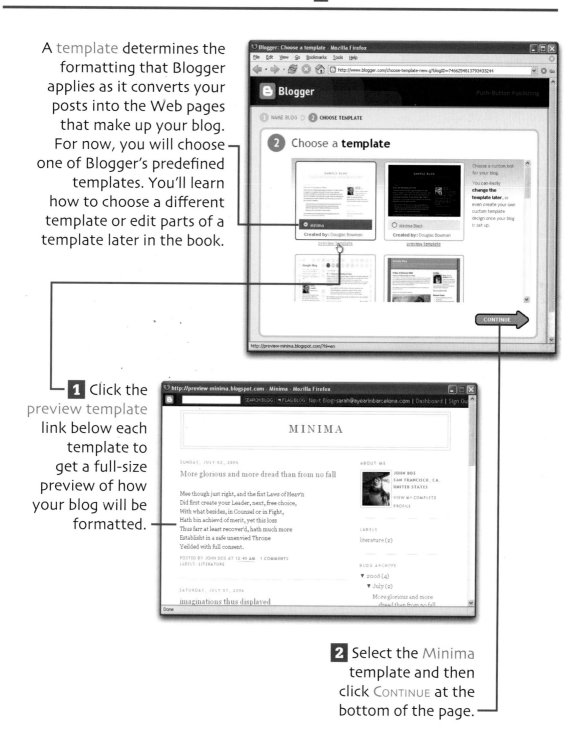

1 Click the preview template link below each template to get a full-size preview of how your blog will be formatted.

2 Select the Minima template and then click CONTINUE at the bottom of the page.

publish your first post

1 Once Blogger has created your blog, you'll get this confirmation note. Click START BLOGGING to display the Posting | New Post window where you can write your first entry.

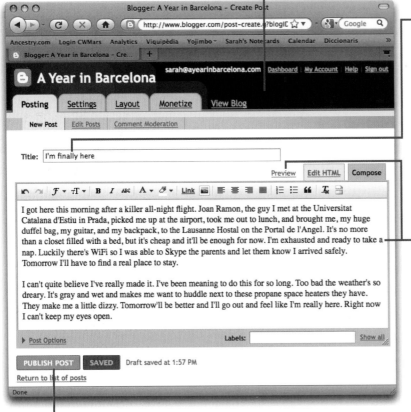

2 The title of your blog post is used to identify your entry both on your main blog page and in the blog archive section.

3 Type your post in the main editing area. If desired, click Preview to get an idea of how it will look once published.

4 Finally, click PUBLISH POST to add your entry to your blog. (We'll add extra formatting and other embellishments a bit later on.)

5 Once your new post has been published, you'll see this confirmation message. Click View Blog to see your brand new blog, and its first entry.

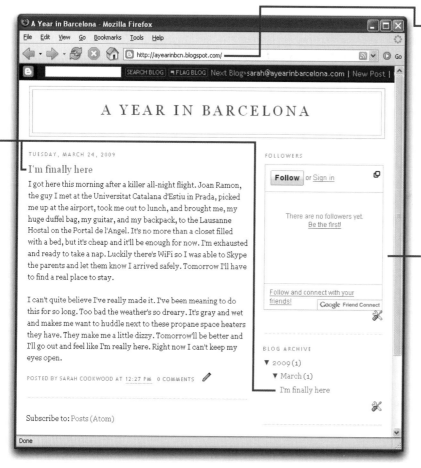

You are now an official blogger! Your new blog is published at the Web address you chose on page 4. By default, it is available to everyone who is on the Internet.

Your blog is automatically formatted with the template you chose on page 5.

the dashboard

If you are signed into your account (which you should
be if you've been following the steps in this chapter),
going to http://www.blogger.com or clicking any
Blogger icon will bring you to the Dashboard.

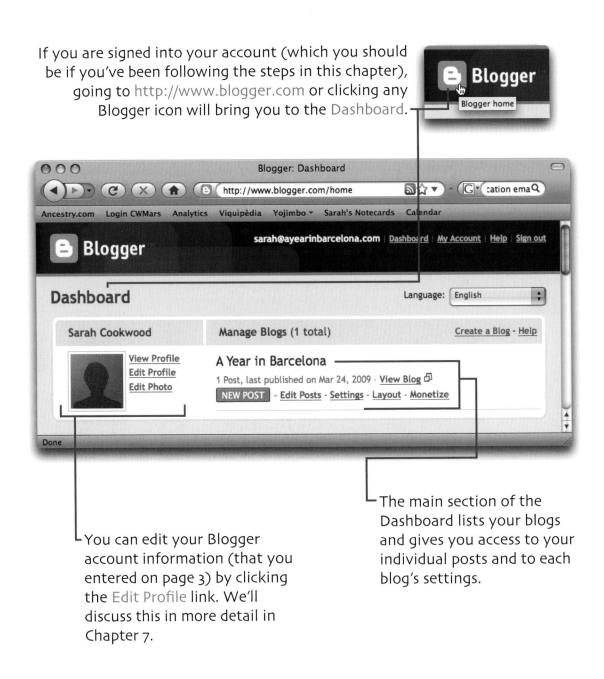

You can edit your Blogger
account information (that you
entered on page 3) by clicking
the Edit Profile link. We'll
discuss this in more detail in
Chapter 7.

The main section of the
Dashboard lists your blogs
and gives you access to your
individual posts and to each
blog's settings.

starting your blog

use the new post editor

Blogger has a new post editor which is (at press time) not yet the default option. It is so great, though, that I'm willing to make you fuss with obscure settings in order to take advantage of it.

1 From the Dashboard (see previous page), click Settings.

Manage Blogs (1 total)

A Year in Barcelona

1 Post, last published on Mar 24, 2009 - <u>View Blog</u>

NEW POST - <u>Edit Posts</u> - <u>Settings</u> - <u>Layout</u> - <u>Monetize</u>

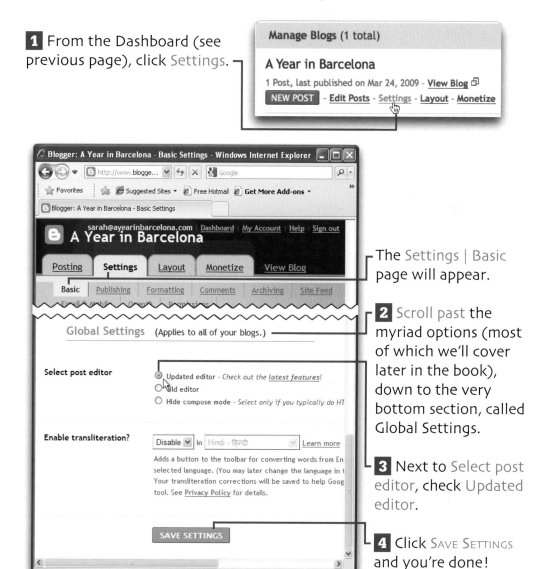

The Settings | Basic page will appear.

2 Scroll past the myriad options (most of which we'll cover later in the book), down to the very bottom section, called Global Settings.

3 Next to Select post editor, check Updated editor.

4 Click SAVE SETTINGS and you're done!

sign out and in

When you are done working on your blog, or would like to see it the way your visitors see it, click the Sign out link at the top-right corner of the Dashboard.

When you are ready to continue with your blog, go to Blogger's home page (by clicking any Blogger icon or typing http://www.blogger.com), enter your Username and Password (that you created on page 3), and then click SIGN IN.

extra bits

set up an account p. 3

- A Google account gives you access to all of Google's services (Blogger, Gmail, Google Groups, etc.), but you have to sign up for each service individually.

- You can sign up for a Google account with a non-Google email address. In that case, the password that you choose for your Google account does not have to match the one you use to retrieve your email.

- If you don't already have an email account, you can create one with Gmail (http://www.gmail.com). Because Gmail is also part of Google, this will automatically create a Google account which you can then also use to sign in to Blogger (though you'll have to accept Blogger's Terms of Service the first time you create a blog).

- If you already have a Google account and have already signed up for Blogger, you can log in, create a new blog from your Dashboard and then follow the rest of the instructions in this chapter to create your new blog.

name your blog p. 4

- While you can have a blog with the same title as someone else's, the Blog address (URL) you choose must be unique. If you happen to type one that's already in use, you'll get an error and a chance to try another.

- You can later delete a blog by choosing Settings | Basic and clicking the Delete blog link at the top of the page.

choose a template p. 5

- If you don't like any of the given templates, don't fret. You'll learn how to choose a different template (from a wider selection) or modify the template according to your own style in Chapter 5.

publish your first post p. 6

- You don't have to create your first post right away. You can sign out as described on page 10 and then after a rest, start from Chapter 2, where you can add a new post on page 14 .

extra bits

the dashboard p. 8

- You can have as many blogs as you like. They will all be listed in the Dashboard and be treated independently by Blogger. They are all identified with the Blogger user name that you created on page 3.

use the new post editor p. 9

- There are several categories of settings and various options under each one. When I write Settings | Basic, that means you have to start from the Settings tab and then click the Basic subtab underneath. It turns out though that the Settings | Basic page automatically comes up when you click Settings in the Dashboard.

- If you can't find the Updated editor option at the bottom of the Settings | Basic page, it's probably because Blogger has made it the default and you don't have to worry about activating it. Yay!

sign out and in p. 10

- If you blog on a public computer, be sure to sign out each time you are done writing your blog. Otherwise, the next person who uses the computer will be able to write entries to your blog or change its settings.

- Click the Remember me box in the Sign In area if you want your browser to save a cookie with your user name and password. When you type the first few letters of your user name, the browser will fill in the rest of the name, and the password as well. Needless to say, this is only a good idea on a private computer.

- If you forget your password, click the question mark next to the word Password in the Sign in area. Blogger will help you retrieve your password and/or user name.

2. writing your blog

Once you've got your blog up and running, you can get down to the real task at hand: writing. In this chapter, you'll learn how to create new entries, edit them, save them as a draft, post them, and finally, delete them.

You'll also learn how to add links, formatting, jump breaks, and labels, change the date and time, and control commenting to your blog entries.

add a new post

1 Click any Blogger icon to go to Blogger's home page. As long as you've signed in with your user name and password (as described on page 10), you'll see the Dashboard—the main control center for your blogs.

2 Click the New Post link under the blog to which you wish to add an entry.

3 The Posting | New Post page appears. This is where you'll compose your blog post.

4 If desired, drag the bottom-right corner to make the edit area larger.

You can also get to this page by clicking New Post in the Posting tab.

writing your blog

5 Type in your blog's title and body.

6 Click PUBLISH POST when you're done.

Your posts are automatically saved every minute.

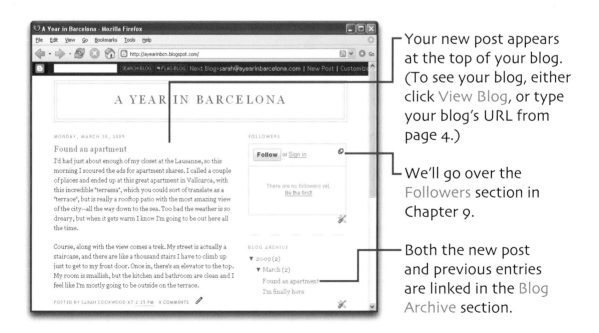

Your new post appears at the top of your blog. (To see your blog, either click View Blog, or type your blog's URL from page 4.)

We'll go over the Followers section in Chapter 9.

Both the new post and previous entries are linked in the Blog Archive section.

edit a post

1 Click Edit Posts under your blog in the Dashboard window (found at Blogger's home page as long as you've signed in with your user name and password).

2 A list of your blog's entries appears. Click the Edit link next to the entry you want to change.

You can also get to this page by clicking Edit Posts in the Posting tab.

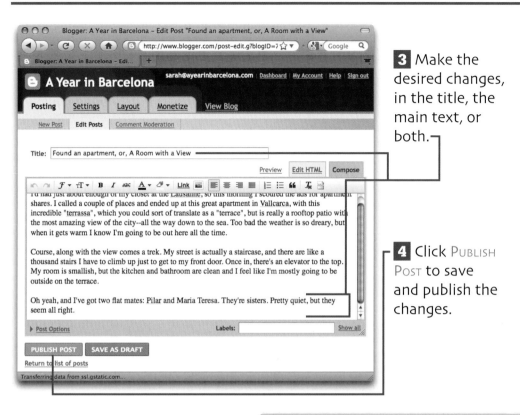

3 Make the desired changes, in the title, the main text, or both.

4 Click PUBLISH POST to save and publish the changes.

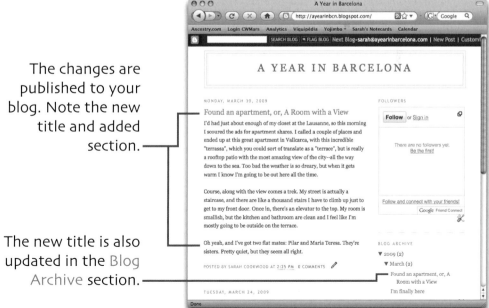

The changes are published to your blog. Note the new title and added section.

The new title is also updated in the Blog Archive section.

add a link

1 First, find the page that you want to link to and copy its URL. If you are linking to a blog post, as shown here, be sure to get the URL of the individual post (called a permalink, and usually found both in the post's title and in its date). To do so, right-click a link to the post (Control-click on a Mac) and choose Copy Shortcut, Copy Link, or whatever it's called in your browser, from the pop-up menu that appears.

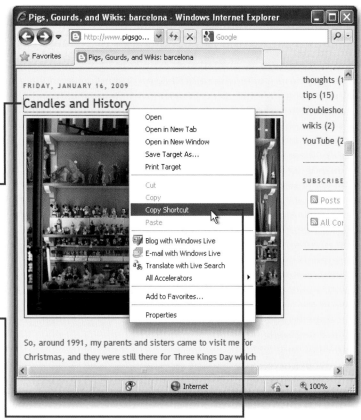

2 In your blog entry, select the text that you want to link from.

Title: A Shop for Every Little Thing

This place is incredible. I had read this blog about how Barcelona has a shop candles - and thought it was a bit of an exaggeration. Today, I walked right out is one of the oldest continuous running stores in Barcelona, and decided

3 Then click the Link tool in the toolbar.

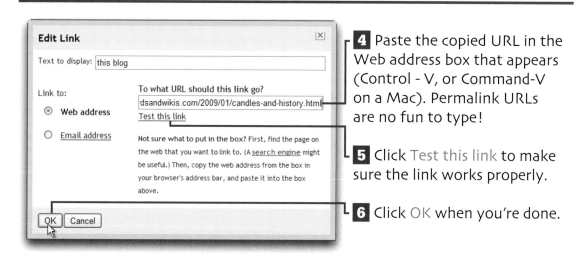

4 Paste the copied URL in the Web address box that appears (Control - V, or Command-V on a Mac). Permalink URLs are no fun to type!

5 Click Test this link to make sure the link works properly.

6 Click OK when you're done.

7 Back in the post editor, when you select any part of the linked text, a strip of link information appears.

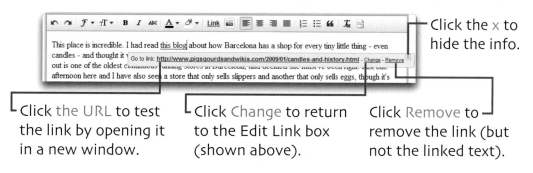

Click the x to hide the info.

Click the URL to test the link by opening it in a new window.

Click Change to return to the Edit Link box (shown above).

Click Remove to remove the link (but not the linked text).

When the entry is published, a click on the linked text will send the visitor to the destination URL on the other blog.

save a draft

1 If you don't quite finish a post, you can *save a draft* of it—thereby delaying its publication on your blog—by clicking SAVE NOW below the main editing area.

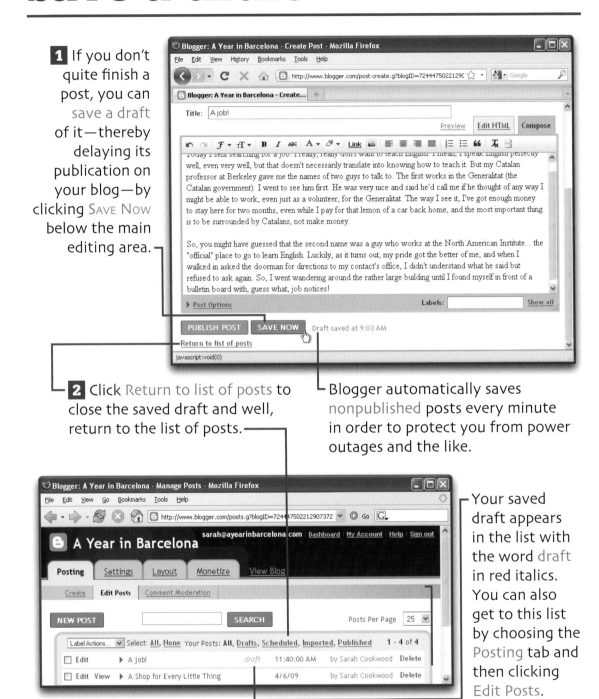

2 Click Return to list of posts to close the saved draft and well, return to the list of posts.

Blogger automatically saves *nonpublished* posts every minute in order to protect you from power outages and the like.

Your saved draft appears in the list with the word *draft* in red italics. You can also get to this list by choosing the Posting tab and then clicking Edit Posts.

publish a draft

1 In the Posting | Edit Posts page (also shown at the bottom of the previous page), click the Edit button next to the draft you wish to publish.

2 Edit the post as desired.

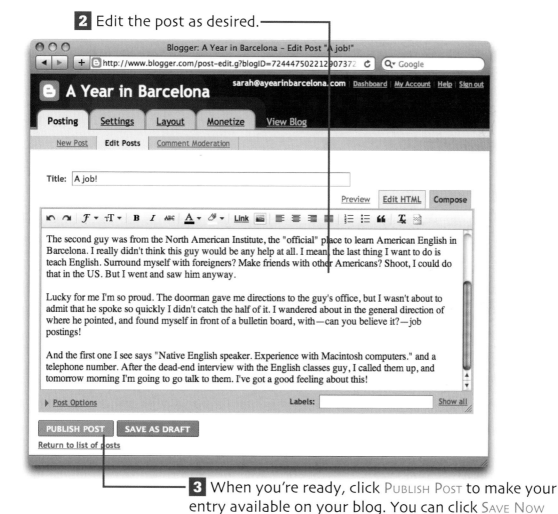

3 When you're ready, click PUBLISH POST to make your entry available on your blog. You can click SAVE NOW again if you're still not ready to publish it.

add formatting

The Compose bar, available on most browsers, offers a variety of formatting tools and wysiwyg display.

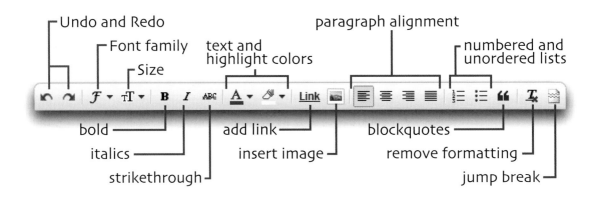

Undo and Redo
Font family
Size
text and highlight colors
paragraph alignment
numbered and unordered lists

bold
italics
strikethrough
add link
insert image
blockquotes
remove formatting
jump break

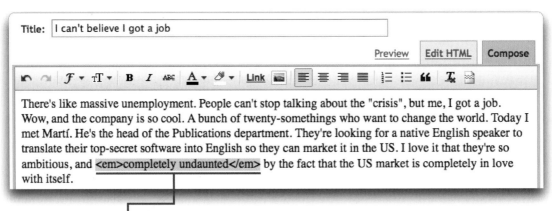

Title: I can't believe I got a job

Preview | **Edit HTML** | **Compose**

There's like massive unemployment. People can't stop talking about the "crisis", but me, I got a job. Wow, and the company is so cool. A bunch of twenty-somethings who want to change the world. Today I met Martí. He's the head of the Publications department. They're looking for a native English speaker to translate their top-secret software into English so they can market it in the US. I love it that they're so ambitious, and <em>completely undaunted</em> by the fact that the US market is completely in love with itself.

You can also add formatting by typing the desired HTML tags around the text you wish to format. You might want to do this with browsers that don't support the Compose bar, or for formatting that the Compose bar does not provide (like, say <h2> or <em>).

1 Select the text that you want to format.

Title: I can't believe I got a job

$\mathcal{F}$ ▾ ᴛT ▾ **B** *I* ᴬᴮᶜ **A** ▾ ✎ ▾ Link 🖼 ▤

There's like massive unemployment. People can't stop talking job. Wow, and the company is so cool. A bunch of twenty-son Today I met Martí. He's the head of the Publications departm speaker to translate their top-secret software into English so t they're so ambitious, and completely undaunted completely in love with itself.

2 Click the desired formatting tool from the Compose bar. I've chosen italics.

Title: I can't believe I got a job

$\mathcal{F}$ ▾ ᴛT ▾ **B** *I* ᴬᴮᶜ **A** ▾ ✎ ▾ Link 🖼 ▤

There's like massive unemployment. People can't stop talking job. *Wow, and the company is so cool*. A bunch of twenty-son Today I met Martí. He's the head of the Publications departm speaker to translate their top-secret software into English so t they're so ambitious, and completely undaunted completely in love with itself.

3 The text is displayed in italics.

WEDNESDAY, APRIL 8, 2009

I can't believe I got a job

There's like massive unemployment. People can't stop talking about the "crisis", but me, I got a job. *Wow, and the company is so cool.* A bunch of twenty-somethings who want to change the world. Today I met Martí. He's the head of the Publications department. They're looking for a native English speaker to translate their top-secret software into English so they can market it in the US. I love it that they're so ambitious, and completely undaunted by the fact that the US market is completely in love with itself.

4 When you preview or publish the post, the text appears with the desired formatting.

writing your blog

add a jump break

If you have a long post, you can insert a jump break to make it easier for visitors to browse through all your posts.

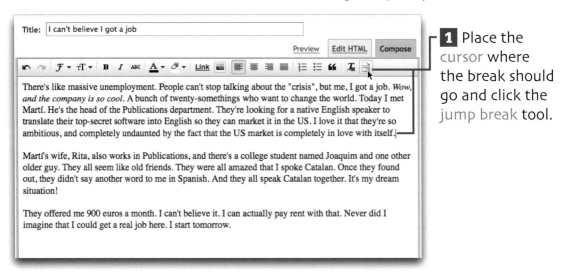

1 Place the cursor where the break should go and click the jump break tool.

2 A gray line shows where the break will occur.

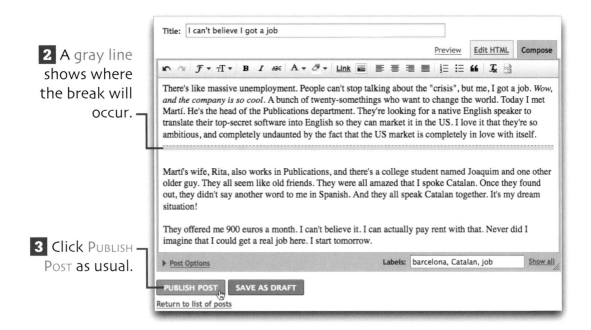

3 Click PUBLISH POST as usual.

writing your blog

If you view the blog's home page, or a summary page (like all the posts in March), only the text before the break is shown.

Visitors must click the Read more » link to view the rest of the post.

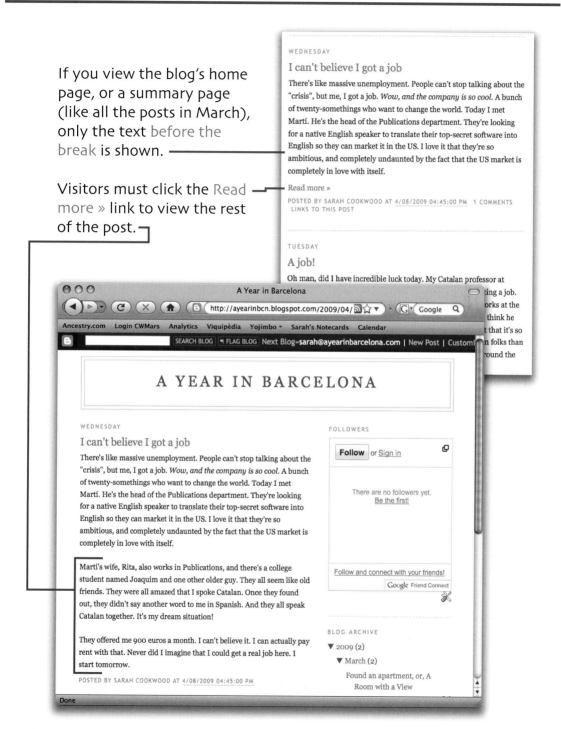

add labels

You can add labels to your posts in order to categorize them and make it easier for your readers to find all your posts about a given topic, say, your job or your family.

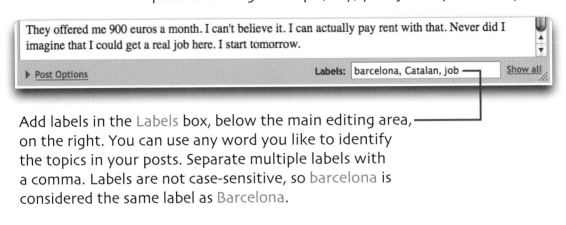

Add labels in the Labels box, below the main editing area, on the right. You can use any word you like to identify the topics in your posts. Separate multiple labels with a comma. Labels are not case-sensitive, so barcelona is considered the same label as Barcelona.

You can also apply labels to existing posts by checking the box next to the post, and choosing the desired label (or New Label) from the Label Actions menu.

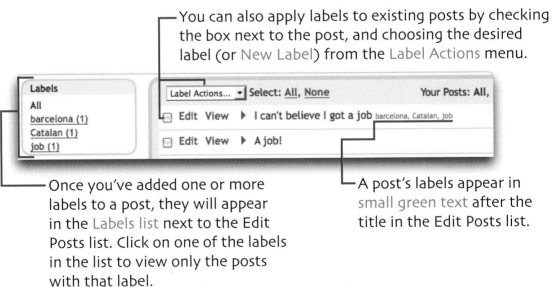

Once you've added one or more labels to a post, they will appear in the Labels list next to the Edit Posts list. Click on one of the labels in the list to view only the posts with that label.

A post's labels appear in small green text after the title in the Edit Posts list.

On page 66, you'll learn how to make a list or cloud of the labels available to your readers.

writing your blog

change the date/time

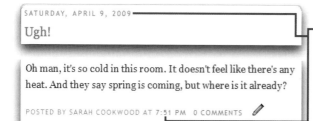

Blogger automatically stamps your posts with the date and time that you first published the post.

1 If you would rather stamp the post with some other day or time, including one in the future, click Post Options at the lower-left of the main editing area.

2 At the right end of the Post options area that appears, enter the desired date and time. You must enter both the hours and the minutes (even if they are :00) or Blogger will ignore the changes.

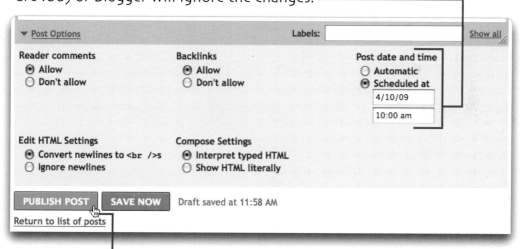

3 Click Publish Post when you're done. If you've chosen a time and date in the future, the post will be saved and then automatically published at the specified time.

control commenting

By default Blogger allows readers to add comments to your blog. All they have to do is click the [#] Comments link at the end of your post.

1 You can control the commenting on each individual post by clicking Post Options below the main editing area.

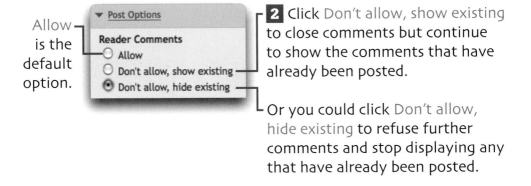

Allow is the default option.

2 Click Don't allow, show existing to close comments but continue to show the comments that have already been posted.

Or you could click Don't allow, hide existing to refuse further comments and stop displaying any that have already been posted.

We'll talk about how to allow only some people to comment on your posts in Chapter 8.

writing your blog

delete a post

1 Go to the Posting | Edit Posts page to see the list of posts in your blog. Then click Delete next to the one you want to get rid of.

2 You'll get one more chance to cancel the deletion. If you're sure, click DELETE IT. It'll disappear from your blog forever.

extra bits

add a new post p. 14

- If you see the generic Blogger home page instead of the Dashboard, you probably have not signed in yet (see page 10).

- You can also get to the Posting | New Post page by clicking NEW POST on the left side of the Posting | Edit Posts page as shown below.

- If the toolbar looks different, it may be that you haven't chosen the Updated editor. See page 9 for details.

edit a post p. 16

- Note that when you're editing an already published post, the post is not saved automatically—and thus the changes aren't published automatically. If you click Save as Draft, your changes are saved but the post is unpublished (removed) from your blog. You'll have to click Publish Post again to republish the post.

add a link p. 18

- If you are adding a link to a regular Web page, you can copy the URL from the Address Bar at the top of the Browser window by selecting it, right-clicking (Control-click on a Mac), and choosing Copy from the pop-up menu that appears.

- Each time you publish a post, Blogger does three things: it adds the new post to your main blog page, it updates the archive page if necessary, and it creates a separate, independent post page whose sole job is to display that new blog post (and any comments and backlinks it may receive). Because the main page of a blog is subject to frequent updating, using the blog's main URL for linking to the current post will only work until a new entry is posted. Instead, if you want to link to a specific blog entry, you should link to the post page, whose URL will not change. Such a link is called a permalink.

- Currently, Blogger creates a permalink out of the title at the beginning of each post and the timestamp in the byline at the end of each post. In older versions of Blogger, the link was labeled Permalink. In some blogging software, permalinks are identified with a hash sign (#).

writing your blog

- If you use a browser that doesn't offer a Link button, or if you use the Edit HTML tab, you can write the link code manually. Type <a href="url"> before the linked text and then </a> after it. It should look something like this:

  <a href="http://www.site.com/target.html">linked text</a>

  Make sure to use straight quotes, and don't forget the http://.

- If you disable post pages on the Settings | Archiving page, your blog's permalinks will change since the post pages will no longer exist. When you disable post pages, Blogger keeps all your current posts on the main page and creates a separate page for each set of archived posts. In this case, if you change the archiving frequency (see page 53), the permalinks will also change.

save a draft p. 20

- Once you publish a post, Blogger won't save the changes automatically (in order to keep readers from viewing your edits in real time). You will notice that the Save Now button changes to Save as Draft. If you choose Save as Draft, Blogger will unpublish your post and thus remove it from your blog. You can republish it by clicking the Publish Post button.

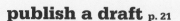

publish a draft p. 21

- You can also remove a post from your blog temporarily by editing it and saving it as a draft.

- Unless you choose otherwise, a post is dated with the day and time it was first published, not when you began writing it (which is how Blogger used to work).

extra bits

add formatting p. 22

- If your Compose bar doesn't look like the one shown, make sure you have followed the steps for updating your post editor on page 9. That said, the Compose bar varies slightly from browser to browser. The one shown is from Internet Explorer 8 for Windows.

- Although the Compose bar is designed to save you from writing HTML, it is perfectly fine to type HTML tags right in there; you don't have to switch to the Edit HTML mode. If you do switch to Edit HTML mode, you'll notice the HTML code stays intact. But when you switch back to Compose, the HTML code will be displayed as if it were in a browser.

- If you need help with HTML, try my bestselling HTML, XHTML, and CSS, Sixth Edition: Visual QuickStart Guide.

- Another reason to use the Edit HTML mode is to adjust the CSS that Blogger applies.

- Did you notice that there's no Video tool or Spell check in this rendition of the Compose bar? By the time you read this, there may be. Blogger is always in a state of flux. Consult the book's web site for more details (see page xii).

change the date/time p. 27

- The Schedule at: label changes to Set Date and Time for posts that have already been published. If you don't have either option, make sure you have updated your post editor as described on page 9.

- Blogger used to date posts with the time and day you first began writing them. Now if you choose the default Automatic option, Blogger will stamp your post with the time and date that it was first published. If you edit the post later, the original time and date of publication are still used.

- If you omit the am/pm from the time, Blogger will assume that you mean am.

- A post's date and time determine its place on your blog. So, to change the order of your posts, change their date and time.

- You can use the Schedule at: box to write posts ahead of time and then have them published at the time and date of your choosing.

delete a post p. 29

- If you're not sure whether or not to delete a post, you can always save it as a draft (page 20) and decide later. Blogger will keep the post in your Edit Posts list, but will unpublish it from your blog.

3. adding multimedia to your blog

Sometimes a picture can illustrate a point much more accurately and creatively than a long blog post. In this chapter, you'll learn how to add images, move them around, and format them.

You'll also learn how to add and embed videos, both yours and those of other people.

Last but not least, you'll see how to add audio to your blog, perhaps in preparation for creating a podcast.

I have to note, especially in this chapter, that Blogger is a bit of a moving target. The software is constantly being updated and improved. Please check the book's web site for any updates (see page xii).

upload images

1 To begin, click the Insert Image tool in the Compose bar.

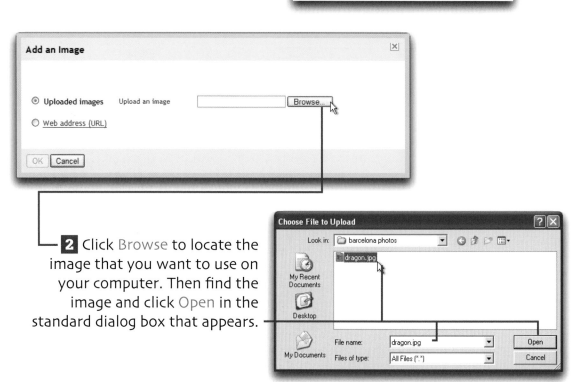

2 Click Browse to locate the image that you want to use on your computer. Then find the image and click Open in the standard dialog box that appears.

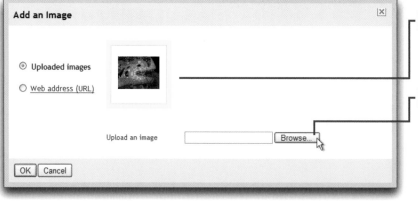

3 A preview of the image appears in the box.

4 Click the Browse button to upload another image.

adding multimedia to your blog

5 The second image now appears in the Add an Image box as well.

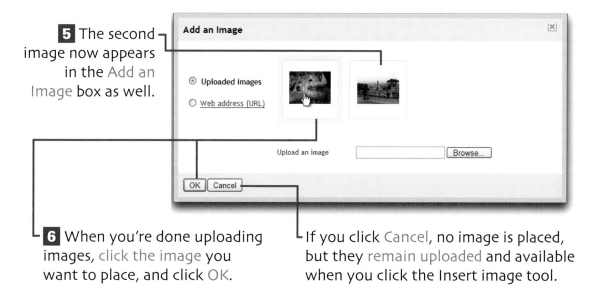

6 When you're done uploading images, click the image you want to place, and click OK.

If you click Cancel, no image is placed, but they remain uploaded and available when you click the Insert image tool.

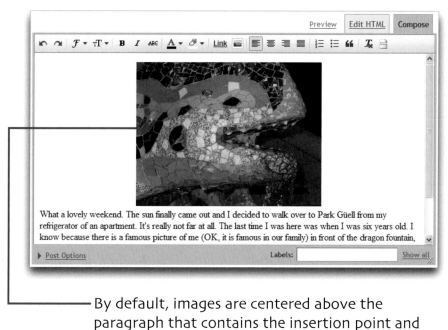

By default, images are centered above the paragraph that contains the insertion point and displayed at Medium size (320 x 240 pixels).

place an(other) image

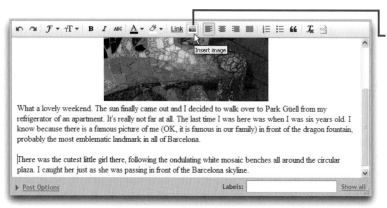

1 To place an additional image, click the Insert image tool again.

2 All of the previously uploaded images will still be visible in the Add an Image box. Click the desired image and click OK.

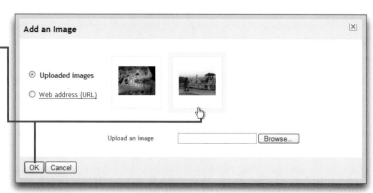

The new image is placed at the insertion point. By default, it is centered and of Medium size (320 x 240 pixels).

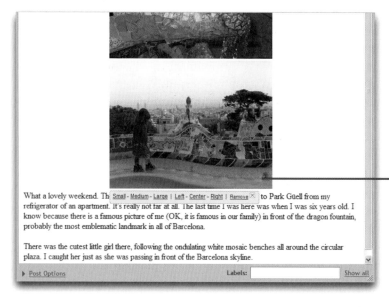

adding multimedia to your blog

move an image

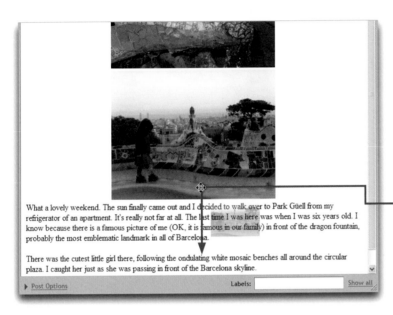

An image is placed above the paragraph with the insertion point by default. You can move it somewhere else by dragging it to a new position.

Drag the image between the two paragraphs.

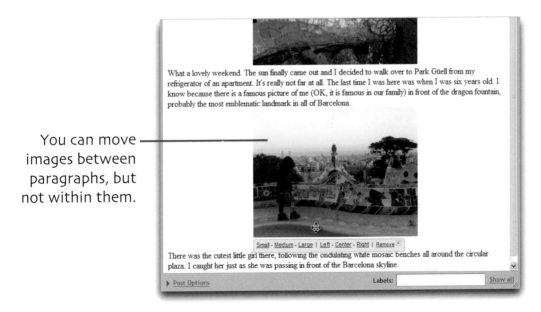

You can move images between paragraphs, but not within them.

wrap text around

The easiest way to wrap text around an image is to drag the image to the left or right part of the paragraph.

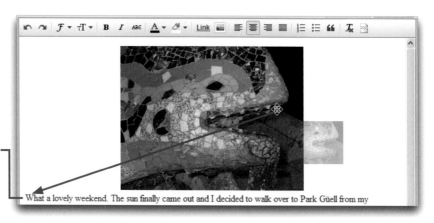

What a lovely weekend. The sun finally came out and I decided to walk over to Park Güell from my

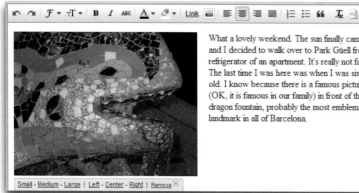

What a lovely weekend. The sun finally came out and I decided to walk over to Park Güell from my refrigerator of an apartment. It's really not far at all. The last time I was here was when I was six years old. I know because there is a famous picture of me (OK, it is famous in our family) in front of the dragon fountain, probably the most emblematic landmark in all of Barcelona.

Small - Medium - Large | Left - Center - Right | Remove ⊠

The text jumps into place on the other side of the image. Blogger takes care of adding a bit of margin around your image as well.

You can also select the image and then choose the alignment option from the options that appear.

Click Right to align the image to the right and wrap the text to the left.

There was the cutest little gi Small - Medium - Large | Left - Center - Right | Remove ⊠ ches all around the circular plaza. I caught her just as she was passing in front of the Barcel a skyline.

Images in Blogger never wrap around each other. One image must "end" before the next one is displayed.

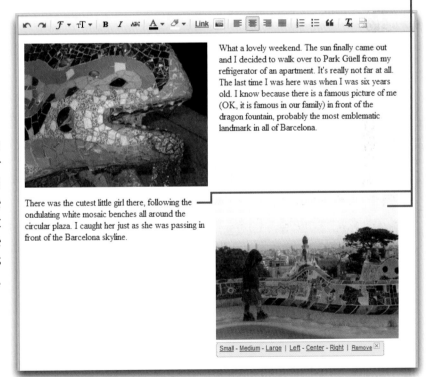

resize an image

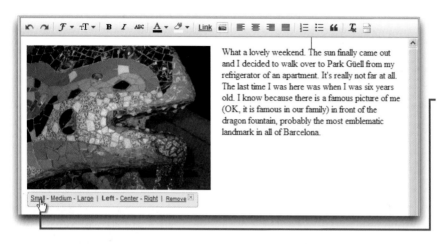

Click Small to reduce the image to 200 x 150 pixels.

The text and the other elements on the page reflow to adjust for the image's new size.

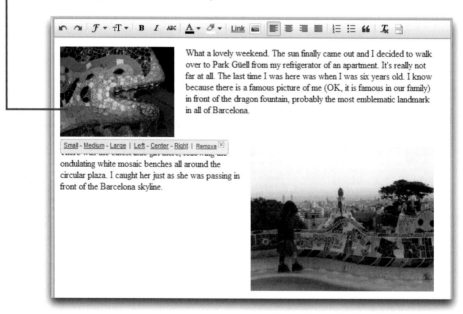

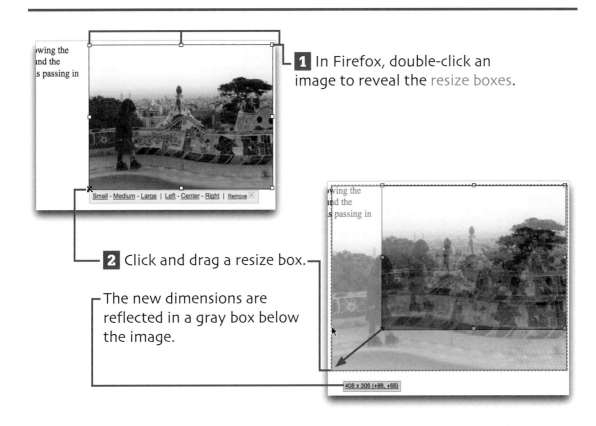

1 In Firefox, double-click an image to reveal the resize boxes.

2 Click and drag a resize box.

The new dimensions are reflected in a gray box below the image.

You can always return to one of Blogger's standard sizes by clicking Small (200 x 150 pixels), Medium (320 x 240), or Large (400 x 300).

remove an image

Click the image to see its controls and then click Remove at the far right.

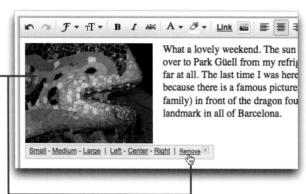

Saturday in the Park Güell

What a lovely weekend. The sun finally came out and I decided to walk over to Park Güell from my refrigerator of an apartment. It's really not far at all. The last time I was here was when I was six years old. I know because there is a famous picture of me (OK, it is famous in our family) in front of the dragon fountain, probably the most emblematic landmark in all of Barcelona.

There was the cutest little girl there, following the ondulating white mosaic benches all around the circular plaza. I caught her just as she was passing in front of the Barcelona skyline.

Once you publish the changes, the deleted image is no longer displayed.

POSTED BY SARAH COOKWOOD AT 8:37 AM   0 COMMENTS

view images on Picasa

When you upload images with the Insert image tool, those images are stored on Google's image storing service, called Picasa Web Albums, under the same user name (and password) you used for Blogger.

└─ To see and manage your photos on Picasa Web Albums, go to http://picasaweb.google.com, and sign in with your Google/Blogger user name and password.

On Picasa Web Albums, you'll find a folder with a Blogger icon and the same name as your blog containing the images that you've uploaded to Blogger. Manage them by clicking the folder and then viewing, naming, or deleting them.

embed YouTube videos

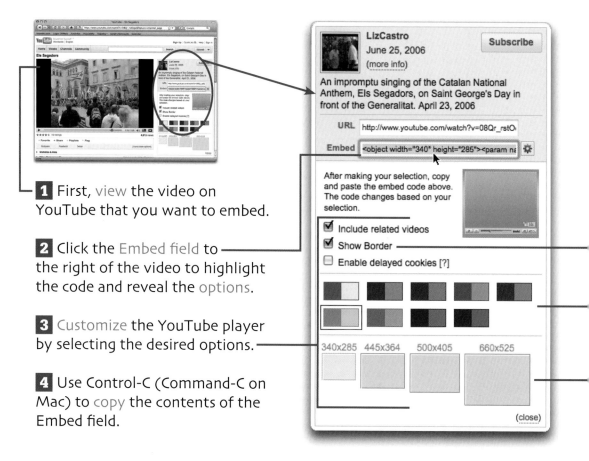

1 First, view the video on YouTube that you want to embed.

2 Click the Embed field to the right of the video to highlight the code and reveal the options.

3 Customize the YouTube player by selecting the desired options.

4 Use Control-C (Command-C on Mac) to copy the contents of the Embed field.

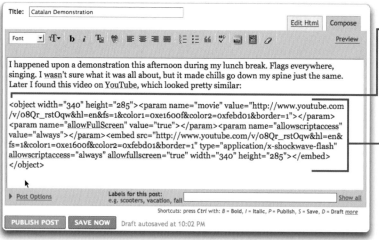

5 Open your blog post and place the cursor where you want the video to appear (by clicking).

6 Use Control-V (or Command-V on the Mac) to paste the embed code into your post. It will be ugly!

This is the sort of border that appears if you select the Show Border option.

You can also choose the color scheme for the border.

Perhaps the most important Embed option is the size of the YouTube player. 340 pixels wide will fit in most Blogger layouts.

MONDAY, APRIL 13, 2009

Catalan Demonstration

I happened upon a demonstration this afternoon during my lunch break. Flags everywhere, singing. I wasn't sure what it was all about, but it made chills go down my spine just the same. Later I found this video on YouTube, which looked pretty similar:

If the Embed field is available at all, it means the uploader of the video has agreed to let people display the video on a web site or blog. Of course, it doesn't guarantee that the content of the video is theirs to share.

add audio

1 Use an audio recording program like Audacity (free and available for both Mac and Windows) to create an audio file and save it in .mp3 format.

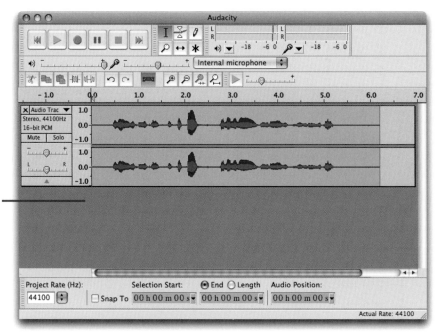

2 You can use an FTP program like CuteFTP or Fetch (shown) to upload the MP3 file to your server. If you're not sure about your server address or capacity, contact your Internet Service Provider.

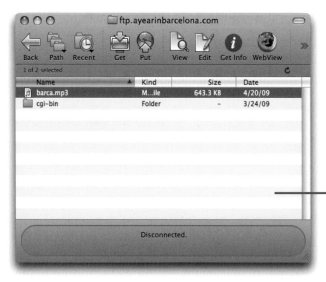

3 Create a link to the sound file by selecting the clickable text and clicking the Link tool.

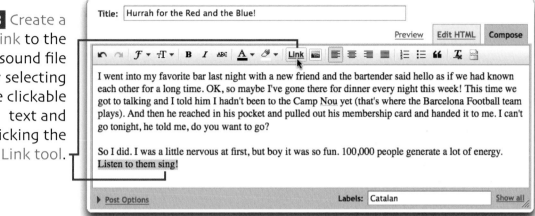

Title: Hurrah for the Red and the Blue!

Preview | Edit HTML | Compose

I went into my favorite bar last night with a new friend and the bartender said hello as if we had known each other for a long time. OK, so maybe I've gone there for dinner every night this week! This time we got to talking and I told him I hadn't been to the Camp Nou yet (that's where the Barcelona Football team plays). And then he reached in his pocket and pulled out his membership card and handed it to me. I can't go tonight, he told me, do you want to go?

So I did. I was a little nervous at first, but boy it was so fun. 100,000 people generate a lot of energy. Listen to them sing!

▶ Post Options | **Labels:** Catalan | Show all

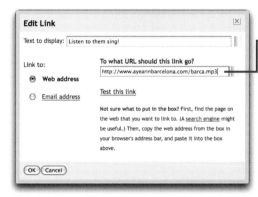

Edit Link

Text to display: Listen to them sing!

Link to:
- ● Web address
- ○ Email address

To what URL should this link go?
http://www.ayearinbarcelona.com/barca.mp3

Test this link

Not sure what to put in the box? First, find the page on the web that you want to link to. (A search engine might be useful.) Then, copy the web address from the box in your browser's address bar, and paste it into the box above.

OK | Cancel

4 Paste in the URL (location on the server) of the MP3 file, and click OK.

5 Once you publish the post, visitors will be able to click the link to hear the audio file.

Hurrah for the Red and the Blue!

I went into my favorite bar last night with a new friend and the bartender said hello as if we had known each other for a long time. OK, so maybe I've gone there for dinner every night this week! This time we got to talking and I told him I hadn't been to the Camp Nou yet (that's where the Barcelona Football team plays). And then he reached in his pocket and pulled out his membership card and handed it to me. I can't go tonight, he told me, do you want to go?

So I did. I was a little nervous at first, but boy it was so fun. 100,000 people generate a lot of energy. Listen to them sing!

POSTED BY SARAH COOKWOOD AT 1:31 PM   0 COMMENTS

extra bits

upload images p. 34

- If you get different looking dialog boxes when you click the Insert image tool, it may be that you haven't yet updated your post editor. Go to page 9 for details.

- Images are always placed directly before the paragraph that contains the insertion point. You'll learn how to move them to other positions on page 37.

- The images you upload are saved in an album on Picasa. See page 43 for more information.

- By default, images are reduced upon upload to a maximum of 1600 x 1200 pixels. You can change the default within the desktop version of Picasa.

- You can upload as many pictures as you want at a time. Only the selected one (with the yellow frame) will be placed when you click OK.

- You can also add images that are already on the Internet. Click Web address (URL) and then enter the URL of the image you want to use. Be sure you have the proper permission.

- The image's URL must end in .jpg, .gif, .png, .tif, or .bmp in order to work properly. Some photo sharing sites (like Picasa) don't make the URL easy to decipher.

- To find the URL of an image on Flickr, click the All Sizes button above the chosen image, and then choose the size that is larger than but closest to the size you want to use in your blog, and scroll down to the field that contains the URL.

- While you can link to photos that are on other servers besides your own, you'll need to get permission to insert photos from sites that do not belong to you.

place an(other) image p. 36

- Images are always inserted above the paragraph that contains the insertion point (and never within a paragraph itself).

move an image p. 37

- Another way to move an image is to click the Edit HTML tab, copy the big ugly chunk of code for the image (it generally starts with <a href="http://3.bp.blogspot.com... and ends with </a>), and paste it in the desired location. Get rid of the extra div tags. (This would be one way to insert an image into the middle of a paragraph.)

- If you drag an image to the right or left of a paragraph, the text in the paragraph will wrap around the image. See page 38 for details.

adding multimedia to your blog

- If you want the image aligned to the left or right without text wrap, you'll have to click the Edit HTML tab and edit the CSS yourself. (Remove the align="center" from the div element and the margins from the image.)

- I could have placed the image where I wanted originally by putting the insertion point before the second paragraph before clicking the Insert image tool. Of course, then I wouldn't have had a good example of moving an image.

wrap text around p. 38

- You can remove text wrap by dragging the image to the center. Also, see the second to last tip in the previous section.

resize an image p. 40

- I'm not sure why this functionality is so different from browser to browser. At any rate, it's a good reason to choose Firefox!

- If you click a corner resize box, the image is scaled proportionately. If you click a side resize box, the image is distorted. You can remove the distortion by choosing one of Blogger's default sizes.

- Blogger no longer shows the size of an image in the code when you click Edit HTML. That doesn't mean you still can't specify the height or width there.

remove an image p. 42

- In Firefox, you can also double-click an image and hit the Delete key to remove it.

- Blogger leaves a bit of HTML detritus behind when you remove an image (both with the Remove link and the Delete key). If you care, or notice weird formatting in your post, you can get rid of it by clicking the Edit HTML tab and then deleting the extra elements (generally <div> elements).

view images on Picasa p. 43

- To be precise, images added with the Insert image tool are stored on Picasa Web Albums, the online portion of Picasa.

- If it hasn't already happened by the time you read this, Picasa may soon be integrated with Blogger's Compose bar. Check the web site for the latest news (see page xii).

extra bits

embed YouTube videos p. 44

- If you can't find the Embed field, it's probably because the person who posted the video has not given permission for the video to be embedded on other web sites. In that case, you can just create a link to it (see page 18 for details).

- Easier ways to upload video are on their way. Check the book's web site for details (see page xii).

add audio p. 46

- When a visitor clicks the link to the audio, their browser opens a helper program (generally Quick-Time on the Mac and Windows Media Player on Windows) to play the sound.

- You can use this same technique to link to any kind of media file, including PDFs, videos you have on your own server, or whatever.

- You can also embed audio into your page but the code is a bit involved. It is described in detail in my book, HTML, XHTML, and CSS: Visual QuickStart Guide, 6th edition.

adding multimedia to your blog

4. personalizing
your blog

Blogger saves your blog entries internally in a database, not as static files. When you hit the Publish Post button, Blogger generates the blog's Web page by outputting the information from the database according to the formatting instructions given in your blog's template, which you originally chose on page 5.

While you can change the template itself (and we'll do just that in Chapter 5), Blogger makes it really easy to edit and adjust, add, remove, and reorder the page elements in your blog, as well as change the fonts and colors used to style it. These are quick and easy ways to give your blog a unique look.

layout settings

To get to the Layout settings from the Dashboard, click Layout under the desired blog.

You can also get to the Layout settings by clicking the Layout tab. Either way, you'll see four subsections: Page Elements, Fonts and Colors, Edit HTML, and Pick New Template.

page elements

The page elements are the building blocks of your blog. There are two default page elements that cannot be removed: the Header (which can contain a title, description, and/or image), and the Blog Posts area (which shows where your blog posts will be displayed). They can be edited, as we will see shortly.

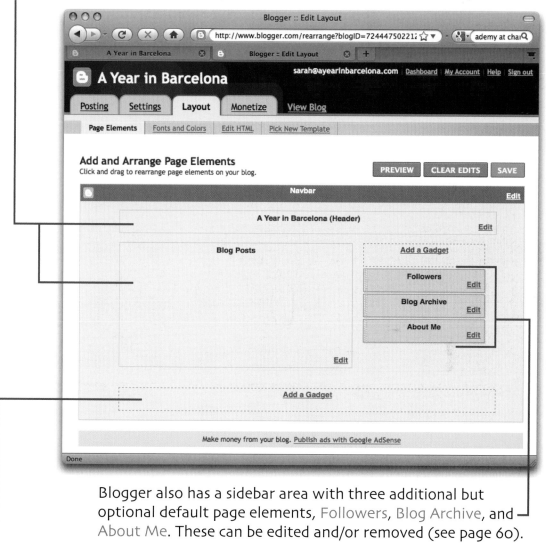

Blogger also has a sidebar area with three additional but optional default page elements, Followers, Blog Archive, and About Me. These can be edited and/or removed (see page 60).

Additional optional page elements (known as gadgets), can be added to your blog layout, as we'll see on page 61.

reorder page elements

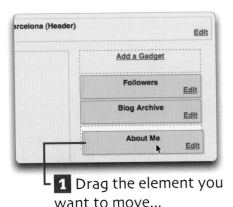

1 Drag the element you want to move...

2 ...and drop it in its new location.

Any page element (or gadget) besides the Header and Blog Posts area can be dragged to a new position, either below the header, above or below the Blog Posts area, anywhere in the sidebar, or anywhere in the footer.

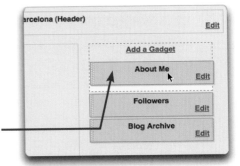

3 Save changes.

4 View the results. Note that the About Me section is now up at the top of the sidebar, and that Followers and Blog Archive come below.

personalizing your blog

add a description

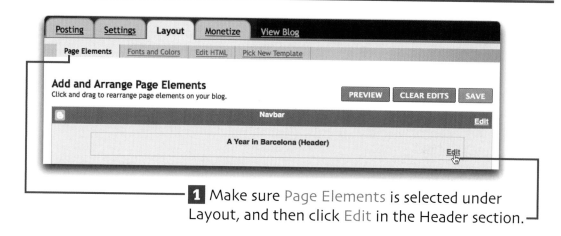

1 Make sure Page Elements is selected under Layout, and then click Edit in the Header section.

2 In the Configure Header box that appears, type the desired Blog Description. Use the description to give your readers an idea of what they'll find in your blog.

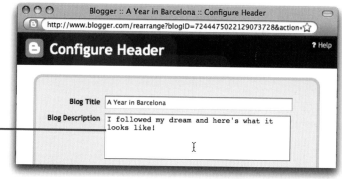

 **3** Click Save to keep the changes.

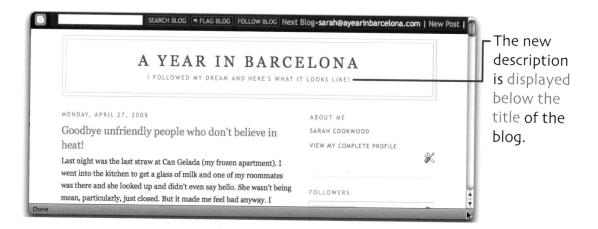

The new description is displayed below the title of the blog.

personalizing your blog

add a header image

1 Return to the Configure Header box (see previous page).

2 Before choosing an image, make sure to check the Shrink to fit box so that Blogger reduces the width of your image to fit the template (and the height proportionately). Otherwise, Blogger will use the original size of your image (and it'll probably be too big).

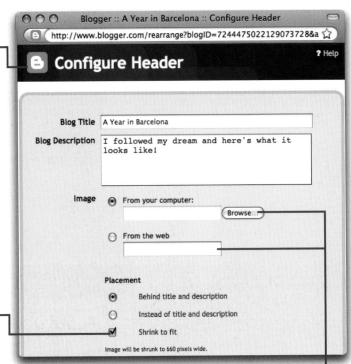

3 Now, choose your header image. You can choose one from your computer by clicking the Browse button, or type in the URL of an image from the Web (being mindful of copyright).

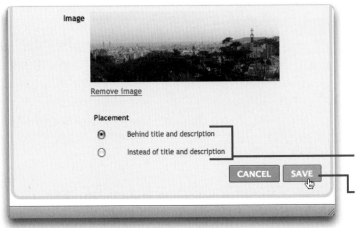

4 Once you've chosen an image, it'll be previewed in the Configure Header box. You can opt to place the image behind the title and description or to display it instead of the title and description.

5 Click Save.

6 If you're going to place an image behind the title and description, be sure that the background is light enough (or has enough contrast) so that the text shows up. You'll learn how to change the color of the text shortly (see page 68).

edit Blog Posts area

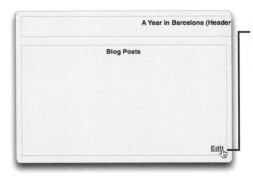

1 You can control how all your blog posts look by adjusting the settings in the Blog Posts area. Click Edit in the bottom right corner to begin.

2 Check (or uncheck) the post date to display (or hide) when a post was written. Choose a date format in the pop-up menu.

3 Check (or uncheck) the Posted by option to show (or hide) who wrote the blog post. Edit the words "Posted by" as desired.

4 Check (or uncheck) the at time box to display (or hide) the time a post was written. Edit the word "at" as needed.

5 Check (or uncheck) the comments box if you want to display (or hide) a link to any comments written about your post. Change the word "comments" as desired.

6 Check (or uncheck) the Links to this post area to show (or hide) links to people who have linked to you. Change the text as desired.

7 Check (or uncheck) the Labels: option to display (or hide) any labels that you've added to categorize your posts. (For more on labels, see page 26.) Change the title as desired.

8 Check (or uncheck) the Show Quick Editing icon to display (or hide) a shortcut to the Editing page for your posts. It's only ever visible to you, not your visitors.

9 Check (or uncheck) the Reactions: area to give your visitors a quick way to comment on your post. You can also edit the choices offered.

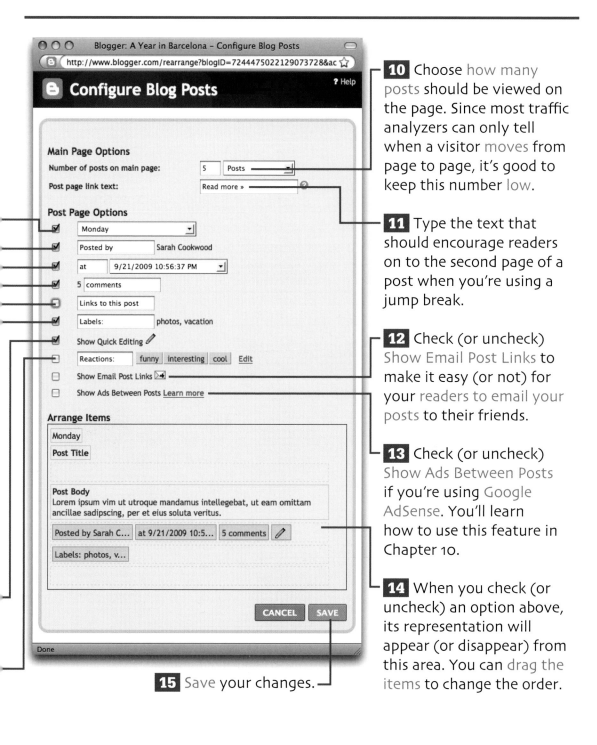

10 Choose how many posts should be viewed on the page. Since most traffic analyzers can only tell when a visitor moves from page to page, it's good to keep this number low.

11 Type the text that should encourage readers on to the second page of a post when you're using a jump break.

12 Check (or uncheck) Show Email Post Links to make it easy (or not) for your readers to email your posts to their friends.

13 Check (or uncheck) Show Ads Between Posts if you're using Google AdSense. You'll learn how to use this feature in Chapter 10.

14 When you check (or uncheck) an option above, its representation will appear (or disappear) from this area. You can drag the items to change the order.

15 Save your changes.

remove a gadget

A gadget is another name for an optional page element, basically any chunk of your blog besides the Header or Blog Posts area. Gadgets can be removed or added at will, making Blogger remarkably customizable.

1 To remove a gadget, begin by clicking its Edit link. We'll remove the Followers gadget since our blog is so new we don't yet have any followers. Later, if desired, when we begin to attract followers, we can return the gadget to the sidebar. ────

2 All gadgets have a Remove button in the lower left corner. Simply click it (and then click OK in the alert that appears) to remove the gadget from your blog layout. ─┐

add a gadget

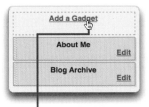

There are many gadgets (remember: optional page elements) that you can add to your Blogger blog. Some are developed by the folks at Blogger and Google, and some by the community at large.

1 To add a new gadget to your page, click Add a Gadget, either in the sidebar or in the footer. Remember you can drag the gadget to a new location once it's created (see page 54).

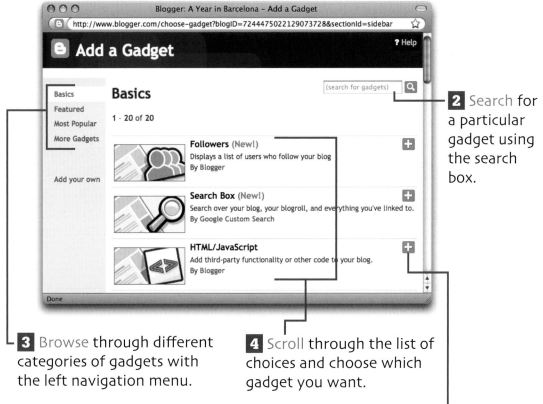

2 Search for a particular gadget using the search box.

3 Browse through different categories of gadgets with the left navigation menu.

4 Scroll through the list of choices and choose which gadget you want.

5 Then click the Plus symbol to add it to your blog. On the next few pages, we'll walk you through adding some specific, useful gadgets.

add a Link List gadget

Link List
Add a collection of your favorite sites, blogs, or web pages.
By Blogger

One useful, basic gadget is the Link List. You'll find it in the Basic category.

1 Click the Plus sign to add the gadget to your blog.

2 The Configure Link List box appears. Type a title for the list. The title will appear as the header in the sidebar.

3 If desired, choose how many links should be shown (though I'm not sure why you'd want to add links and not show them).

Blogger : A Year in Barcelona :: Configure Link List

http://www.blogger.com/rearrange?blogID=7244475022129073728&sectionI

Configure Link List   ? Help

BACK   CANCEL   SAVE

Title   Barcelona

Number of links to show in list   *Leave blank to show all links*

Sorting   Don't Sort

New Site URL   http://www.bcn.cat/en/ihome.htm

New Site Name   City of Barcelona

ADD LINK

BACK   CANCEL   SAVE

javascript:void(0)

4 To add the links themselves, type or paste the URL for the link in the New Site URL box. Then label the link with the New Site Name box. Then click Add Link. Repeat as necessary. The new links will appear in the lower area of the box.

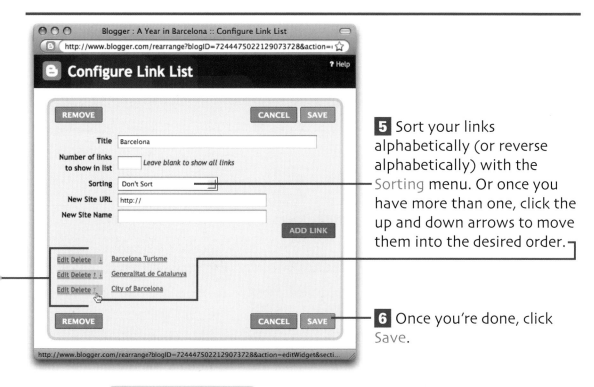

5 Sort your links alphabetically (or reverse alphabetically) with the Sorting menu. Or once you have more than one, click the up and down arrows to move them into the desired order.

6 Once you're done, click Save.

7 Once you save the Link List configuration, the gadget will appear in the Layout | Page Elements page. Drag the gadget to its new desired location as we did on page 54. In this example, I've dragged it between the About Me and Blog Archive gadgets.

8 View the new Link List on your blog. Notice that the header, "Barcelona", comes from the title of the Link List.

personalizing your blog

add Slideshow gadget

1 Once again, click the Add a Gadget link to begin.

2 Find the Slideshow gadget in the Basic section and click the Plus symbol to add it to your blog.

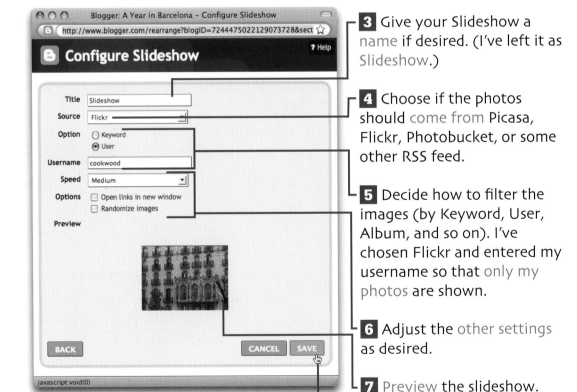

3 Give your Slideshow a name if desired. (I've left it as Slideshow.)

4 Choose if the photos should come from Picasa, Flickr, Photobucket, or some other RSS feed.

5 Decide how to filter the images (by Keyword, User, Album, and so on). I've chosen Flickr and entered my username so that only my photos are shown.

6 Adjust the other settings as desired.

7 Preview the slideshow.

8 Click Save when you're satisfied.

9 If desired, drag the new Slideshow gadget to your desired location. I want it below the About Me gadget.

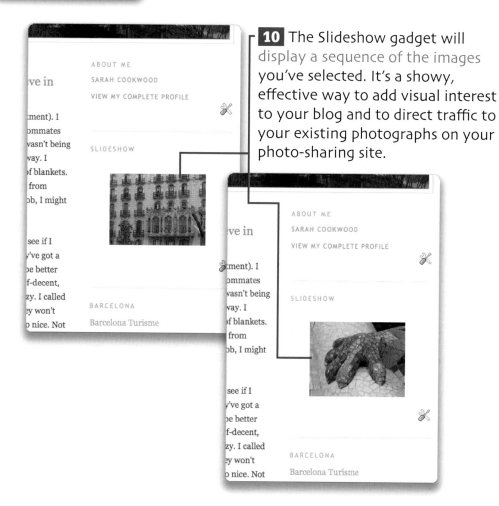

10 The Slideshow gadget will display a sequence of the images you've selected. It's a showy, effective way to add visual interest to your blog and to direct traffic to your existing photographs on your photo-sharing site.

add Labels gadget

Back on page 26, you learned how to add labels to your posts to help your readers find topics of interest more quickly. Here we'll add a Labels list so they can quickly jump to the category of posts they're interested in.

1 Begin by clicking Add a Gadget in the Layout Settings area, and then clicking the Plus symbol next to Labels in the list. ——

2 Give your Labels list a title. This title will be the header in the sidebar. ——

3 Choose Alphabetically next to Sorting so that visitors can easily find the category they're interested in. Use By Frequency if you want to give quick access to popular categories.

4 Choose List next to Display to show a simple list of labels. The Cloud option (shown next page) is good for giving a visual representation of a large collection of labels.

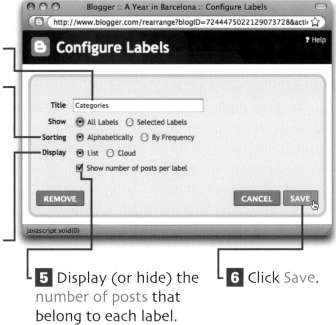

5 Display (or hide) the number of posts that belong to each label.

6 Click Save.

7 Drag the new gadget to the desired spot in the sidebar (or other location, as you prefer).

8 Save the changes in the Layout settings area.

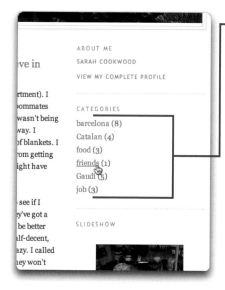

The new Categories section appears in the sidebar with the labels from your posts converted into links. Clicking a label displays all the posts categorized with that label.

A cloud displays each label at a size that reflects how often that label is used. Since showing the number of posts per label would be redundant, I unchecked that option for this example.

personalizing your blog

change colors

1 You can give your blog a distinctive look by changing the color scheme. Start by choosing the Fonts and Colors tab under Layout.

2 A list of types of text appears in the list at left. Choose the one that you want to modify.

3 Then select a new color from the palettes to the right. Blogger gives you a list of colors already used in your blog, a list of colors that match your blog, a larger set of colors, and a box in which you can specify the hex value of any color you need.

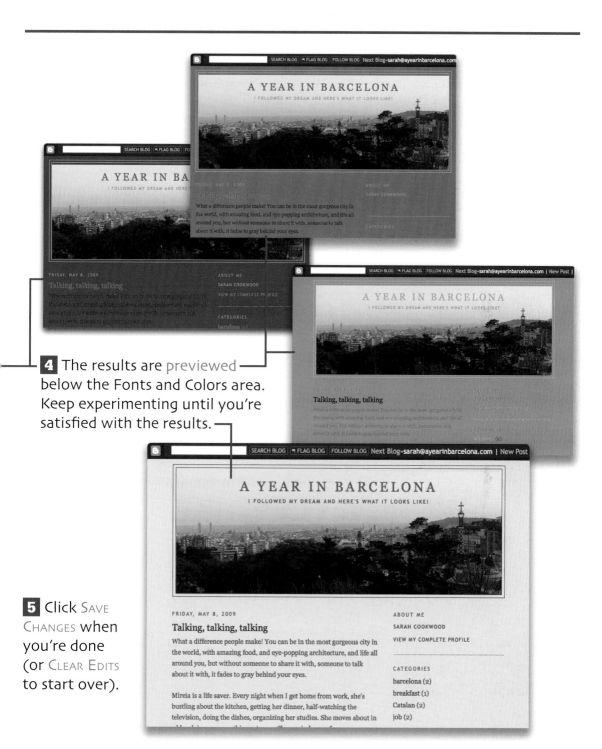

4 The results are previewed below the Fonts and Colors area. Keep experimenting until you're satisfied with the results.

5 Click SAVE CHANGES when you're done (or CLEAR EDITS to start over).

personalizing your blog

change fonts

The text in your blog is divided into categories, some of which are maddeningly overarching while others are perfectly specific. In the Minima template, they are Text Font, Sidebar Title Font, Blog Title Font, Blog Description Font, and Post Footer Font. (In addition, they don't match the color choice names.) You can choose a font, a style, and a size for each one of these categories, but as noted, some overlap.

1 To begin, make sure Fonts and Colors is chosen in the Layout section.

2 Scroll down in the list of items in the Fonts and Colors box and choose one of the types of text for which you can choose font styles.

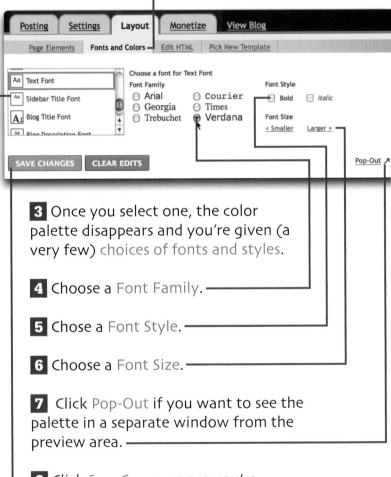

3 Once you select one, the color palette disappears and you're given (a very few) choices of fonts and styles.

4 Choose a Font Family.

5 Chose a Font Style.

6 Choose a Font Size.

7 Click Pop-Out if you want to see the palette in a separate window from the preview area.

8 Click SAVE CHANGES once you're satisfied (or CLEAR EDITS to start over).

9 Select Blog Title Font to change the style of this text. Font Size and Font Style both work as expected: only on this text.

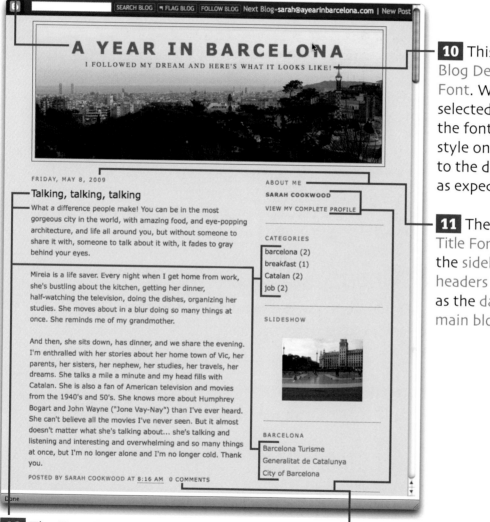

10 This is the Blog Description Font. When selected, changing the font, size, or style only applies to the description, as expected.

11 The Sidebar Title Font controls the sidebar headers as well as the date in the main blog area.

12 The Text Font option (annoyingly) controls the font and italics of the body of the blog, its title, and the text in the Sidebars. Bold formatting is applied only to the body and sidebar text. And Font Size is applied to all the text in your blog! (For relief, see page 80.)

13 The Post Footer Font controls the format of the footer (which contains who wrote the post, and when) and some parts of the sidebars, strangely enough.

change date display

There are a couple of important date settings that you should adjust early on.

1 Begin by choosing the Formatting tab from the Settings section.

2 Choose how you want the date displayed above blog posts with the Date Header Format. If you post frequently, you might just choose the day of the week.

3 If you remove the date, month, and year from the Date Header, you might want to include it in the Footer, which is where the Timestamp Format is used.

4 Finally, choose the Time Zone that matches your location. (The default is PST, or California time.)

Now the header above the blog post shows just the day of the week, the full date is in the footer, and the time is adjusted for where the blog was written.

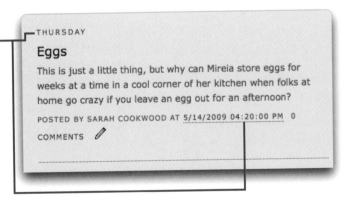

THURSDAY

Eggs

This is just a little thing, but why can Mireia store eggs for weeks at a time in a cool corner of her kitchen when folks at home go crazy if you leave an egg out for an afternoon?

POSTED BY SARAH COOKWOOD AT 5/14/2009 04:20:00 PM 0

COMMENTS 🖉

archive daily

By default, the Blog Archive is organized by months, with individual blog entries listed below each month.

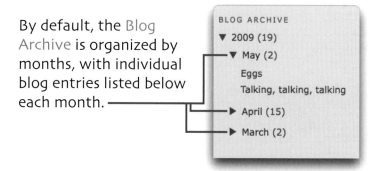

In the Settings | Archiving page, choose the desired option for Archive Frequency. If you blog often, choose Daily or Weekly. If you blog once in a while, it makes more sense to choose Monthly.

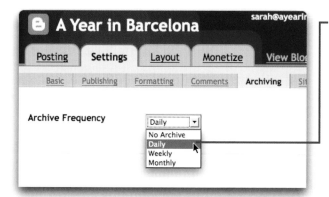

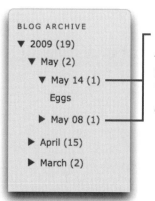

If you choose Daily, the Blog Archive sprouts submenus that show the blog posts from each individual day (as you would expect).

extra bits

reorder page elements p. 54

- You're not limited to dragging new page elements to the sidebar. You can add new gadgets below the Header (that is, across both columns), above or below the Blog Posts area (just one column), or in the footer (across both columns again), as well as anywhere within the sidebar.

add a description p. 55

- You can put a maximum of 500 characters in the Description field.

add a header image p. 56

- The images you upload for your header are stored in the Picasa Web Album. You can see them by going to picasaweb.google.com and choosing your blog name.

edit Blog Posts area p. 58

- Many of the settings in the Blog Posts area can also be changed by choosing options on the Settings | Formatting page.

remove a gadget p. 60

- The Followers gadget can be a great tool for encouraging community later on, but when you don't have any followers, it looks a little needy.

- You can always restore the Followers gadget to your sidebar by following the instructions on page 61.

add a gadget p. 61

- Be sure and test any non Blogger or non-Google gadgets carefully. I have found quite a few of the ones created by the community to be less than perfect.

add a Link List gadget p. 62

- The Link List gadget is great for pure links to other web sites. If you're interested in creating a blog roll, use the Blog List gadget instead. It'll let you display snippets of the blogs themselves, updates of latest blog postings and more. You'll find Blog List in the Basic section of Blogger's gadgets.

add Slideshow gadget p. 64

- You can use the RSS feed feature to customize the group of photos that you link to on Flickr. For more details, see http://bit.ly/xrBi3.

5. working with templates

A Blogger template is the set of rules that describes how each chunk of the blog should be formatted and laid out. Blogger offers many free templates from within Blogger, and there are a number of free Blogger templates available from other sites as well.

While Blogger has made it really easy to tweak templates by adding gadgets or changing colors and fonts as we saw in the last chapter, it also lets you go in and change the actual code of the template itself.

pick a new template

1 Blogger offers a collection of beautiful, professionally designed, CSS-based templates. To choose a new one, go to the Layout | Pick New Template page.

2 A list of templates will appear. Find the one you like best. I've chosen Rounders 3. Click the preview template button to see how your blog will look before making the changes public or permanent.

3 Click SAVE TEMPLATE to save the changes once you're satisfied.

4 When you click View blog, you'll see your blog with the same content, but with the new template's format. What a difference! This is the magic of CSS.

Apart from obvious differences in color, font, and size, there are also placement changes. Note, for example, that there are two sidebar sections with different background colors and contents. It's also clear that we'll have to change the color of the Blog title and description to make them stand out more. And the header image is too narrow.

working with templates

There are lots of Blogger templates available, both through Blogger and through independent sites. Choose the one that best fits your content and your style. You can then edit and adjust the template to your liking as you'll see in the rest of this chapter.

adjust a new template

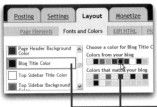

1 In the Fonts and Colors box, choose an appropriate color for the Blog Title Color. (For more details, see page 68.)

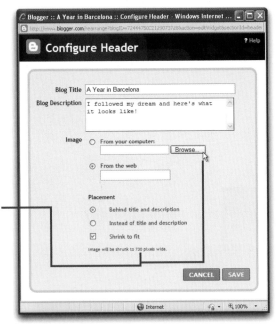

2 Go back to the Configure Header box, remove the existing image, and add it again so that this time it will be shrunk to the width that this template requires (730 pixels in this example). For full instructions, see page 56.

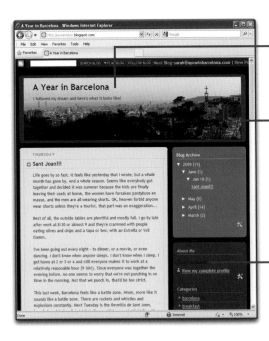

Now we can read the Blog description and title, and the header image fits across the entire box.

Notice, however, that the new color for the Blog title has also affected some of the text in the bottom sidebar. We'll fix that in the next few pages.

working with templates

edit a template

A Blogger template specifies how your blog entry should be translated into HTML (or XHTML) and which formatting—written in the standard Cascading Style Sheet (CSS) language—should be applied to it. You can make changes to the template by editing its code.

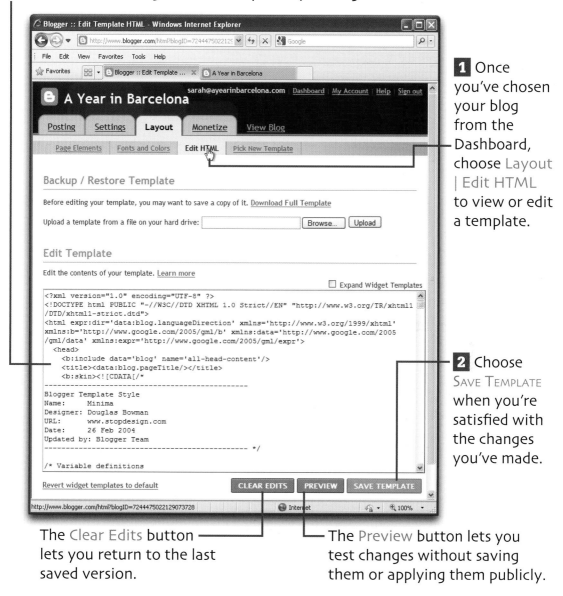

1 Once you've chosen your blog from the Dashboard, choose Layout | Edit HTML to view or edit a template.

2 Choose SAVE TEMPLATE when you're satisfied with the changes you've made.

The Clear Edits button lets you return to the last saved version.

The Preview button lets you test changes without saving them or applying them publicly.

add a variable

It turns out that the Rounders 3 template that we chose on page 76 has a variable (or definition) for the text in the top (green) sidebar, but not for the text in the bottom (blue) sidebar, which instead gets its color from the Blog title. We'll create a new variable for the text color in the bottom sidebar so we can set the two colors independently.

```
<Variable name="topSidebarBgColor"
          description="Top Sidebar Background Color"
          type="color" default="#586" value="#558866">
<Variable name="topSidebarTextColor" description="Top Sidebar Text Color"
          type="color" default="#fff" value="#ffffff">

<Variable name="bottomSidebarTextColor" description="Bottom Sidebar Text Color"
          type="color" default="#fff" value="#ffffff">

<Variable name="topSidebarLinkColor" description="Top Sidebar Link Color"
          type="color" default="#fff" value="#ffffff">
<Variable name="topSidebarVisitedLinkColor"
```

Revert widget templates to default   CLEAR EDITS   PREVIEW   SAVE TEMPLATE

1 On the Layout | Edit HTML page you'll see the contents of the template, written in HTML, CSS, and also Blogger's own code. The variable definitions are generally listed at the top and correspond to the elements that appear in the Fonts and Colors box. I've created the new "bottomSidebarTextColor" variable (using the "topSidebarTextColor" variable immediately above as a guide).

```
#sidebarbottom-wrap1 {
   background:$titleBgColor url("http://www.blogblog.com/rounders3
/corners_side_top.gif") no-repeat $startSide top;
   margin:0 0 15px;
   padding:10px 0 0;
   color: $titleTextColor;
}
```

2 Find the rule where you want to apply the new variable. In this case, it's the one for color under the selector #sidebarbottom-wrap1.

3 Replace $titleTextColor with the name of our new variable (preceded by a dollar sign): $bottomSidebarTextColor. You'll choose the color itself on the next page.

```
#sidebarbottom-wrap1 {
   background:$titleBgColor url("http://www.blogblog.com/rounders3
/corners_side_top.gif") no-repeat $startSide top;
   margin:0 0 15px;
   padding:10px 0 0;
   color: $bottomSidebarTextColor;
}
```

use a new variable

1 Click Layout | Fonts and Colors. ⎯⎯⎯⎯⎯⎯⎯⎯⎯⎯⎯⎯⎯

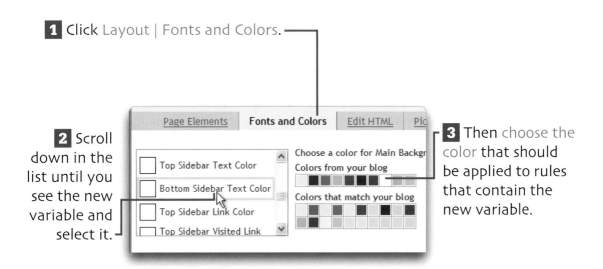

2 Scroll down in the list until you see the new variable and select it. ⎯

3 Then choose the color that should be applied to rules that contain the new variable.

Now the text in the bottom sidebar is white, as defined by the new variable in the Fonts and Colors box, instead of the same blue as the blog description.

back up a template

Once you start making changes to a template, it's a good idea to keep backup copies of it.

To backup a template, go to Layout | Edit HTML and click the Download Full Template link at the top of the window. You'll be prompted to save the file on your computer. You can view and even edit the resulting XML file with any text editor (and you'll probably want to change its name).

You can upload a saved template to use with Blogger from your computer (or a web site) by clicking the Browse button and choosing the desired file. Then click Upload.

working with templates

extra bits

pick a new template p. 76

- When you pick a new template, the old template—and any changes you might have made to it—are lost. If you've made changes to the old template, you may want to back it up first (page 82).

- You don't have to limit yourself to the templates that Blogger provides. Try googling Blogger templates and see what you find. If you decide on an external Blogger template, you'll load it by following the instructions at the bottom of page 82.

- When you go to the Layout | Page Elements page, you'll find that the page elements will differ according to the layout you've chosen. For example, since the Rounders 3 template has two sidebars, you'll see two sidebar page elements—and be able to add gadgets to both of them—on the Page Elements page.

- Note that when you switch to any Rounders template, your existing sidebar page elements will be divided into two groups. The bottommost gadget will go into the top sidebar and all the other gadgets will go into the other sidebar. You may want to adjust this more to your liking. For more details on reorganizing gadgets, see page 54.

adjust a new template p. 78

- It's pretty usual to have to adjust the colors, fonts, and header image after applying a new template. You may also wish to reorder your gadgets and other page elements. (See page 54 for details.)

- Header images are shrunk to fit each given template. For example, headers for the Minima template are shrunk to 660 pixels wide while headers for the Rounders 3 template are shrunk to 730 pixels wide. The easiest solution is to remove the image and place it again to reshrink it to the proper width.

edit a template p. 79

- If you're comfortable with HTML and CSS, you can go right in and edit the code in the template. If you need some help, try consulting my bestselling HTML, XHTML, and CSS, Sixth Edition: Visual Quick-Start Guide. It's a perfect reference for deciphering a template.

extra bits

- Blogger templates also contain Blogger-specific variables and tags. The Blogger tags are not immediately obvious as they are hidden inside widgets. You can display them by clicking the Expand Widget Templates button just above the box that contains the template. You can find more info about variables at http://bit.ly/BloggerVariables and on page 80. You can find more details about template tags here: http://bit.ly/BloggerTemplate.

add a variable p. 80

- Remember there are two steps to adding a variable. First you define the variable, then you must apply it to some CSS rule in the template so that it affects some part of your blog.

- How do you know what CSS rule applies to which part of the blog? While viewing your blog, choose View Source. This will display the HTML code for your blog page. Then search for some text in a given section of your blog. Look at the name of the HTML element that contains the text (or sometimes the class or id of that element). Then go back to the template and find the CSS rule for that element.

- You don't have to use variables to change the fonts or colors. If you feel more comfortable, you can skip the variables altogether and just add the desired font or color to the appropriate CSS rule. The disadvantage is that you won't be able to use the Fonts and Colors box to preview the changes.

- Conversely, if the template you're using only uses CSS fonts and colors to define how each element should look, you can make it easier to edit your blog by adding and applying variables instead.

use a new variable p. 81

- Once you create a variable, it should appear in the Fonts and Colors box. Then you can set a new font and color and preview the effect without saving or publishing the changes.

working with templates

6. blogging from afar

In Chapter 2, you learned how to publish blog posts with your web browser through Blogger's web site. In this chapter, you'll learn how to add posts to your blog from your phone, from your email program, or from your browser's toolbar.

set up SMS blogging

1 You can authorize your phone to send SMS (text messages) to your blog by going to the Settings | Email & Mobile page and then clicking the Add mobile device link at the bottom of the page.

2 Blogger will display the authorization code (in this example: pajgtwpgm).

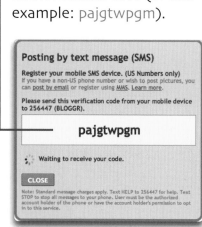

3 Go to the SMS program on your phone and send the authorization code to BLOGGR (256447).

4 You will get a confirmation both on your phone and on your computer. Now you're ready to blog via SMS.

blog via SMS

1 You're out in the field and you find something you have to blog about. Open your SMS program and send your message to BLOGGR (256447).

2 Your SMS is immediately posted to your blog.

set up MMS blogging

1 You can authorize your phone to send MMS (text messages with multimedia) to your blog by going to the Settings | Email & Mobile page and clicking Add mobile device as shown in step 1 on page 86.

2 By default, Blogger will give you the authorization code for SMS. Click the MMS link to get the MMS authorization.

Posting by text message (SMS)

Register your mobile SMS device. (US Numbers only)
If you have a non-US phone number or wish to post pictures, you can post by email or register using MMS. Learn more.

3 Blogger will display the MMS authorization code (in this example: tgpjmgwj).

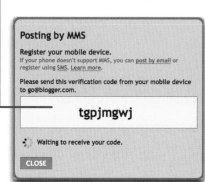

Posting by MMS

Register your mobile device.
If your phone doesn't support MMS, you can post by email or register using SMS. Learn more.

Please send this verification code from your mobile device to go@blogger.com.

tgpjmgwj

⋮ Waiting to receive your code.

CLOSE

4 Go to the MMS program on your phone and send the authorization code to go@blogger.com.

5 You will get a confirmation both on your phone and on your computer. Now you're ready to blog via MMS.

Success! Your mobile phone was verified. Send messages to go@blogger.com to post to your blog.

Registered Devices

The following devices are ready for posting:
5554447373@mms.att.net (MMS)
1 555 444 7373 (SMS)
Add

Messages sent to 256447 (BLOGGR) or go@blogger.com will be posted to the blog: A Year in Barcelona

EDIT SETTINGS   CLOSE

blog via MMS

1 Create a new MMS addressed to go@blogger.com.

2 Click the camera icon (or equivalent on your phone) to add a photo. (Repeat as desired.)

3 Add a text message if desired.

4 Send the message.

5 Your MMS is immediately posted to your blog. (Blogger currently adds a title of Multimedia message to your post. Ew.)

set up email blogging

1 After selecting your blog in the Dashboard, click the Settings tab and then click Email & Mobile.

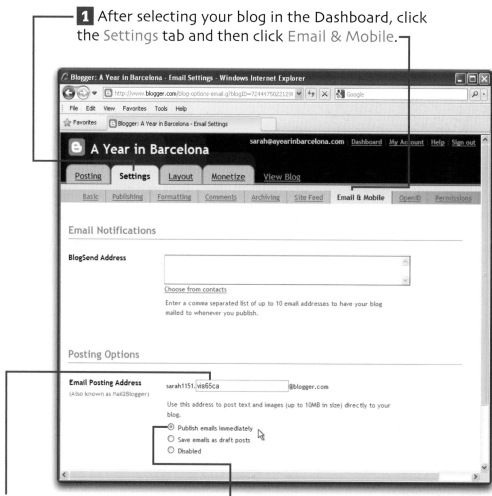

2 Add a secret code to your already encoded user name in order to create the special email address to which you will mail your blog entries.

3 If you want entries to be published as soon as they are received by Blogger, check the Publish emails immediately button. Or check Save emails as draft posts and then manually publish them later.

4 Click Save Settings at the bottom of the window when you're done.

blog via email

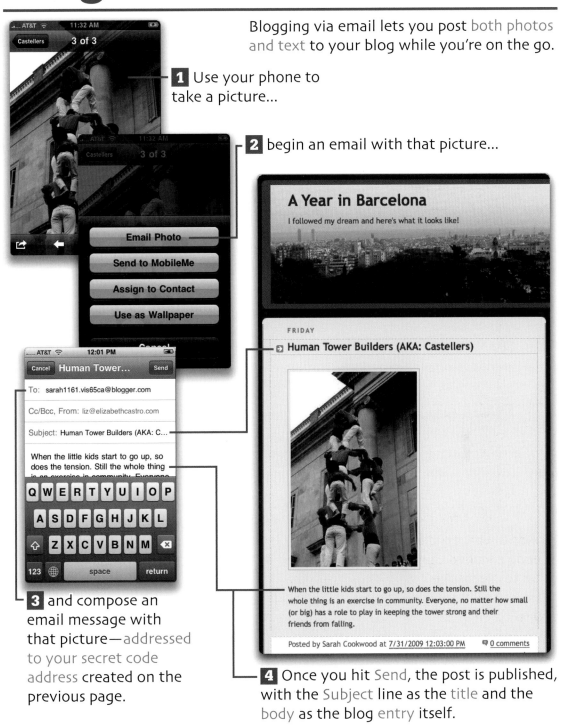

Blogging via email lets you post both photos and text to your blog while you're on the go.

1 Use your phone to take a picture...

2 begin an email with that picture...

3 and compose an email message with that picture—addressed to your secret code address created on the previous page.

4 Once you hit Send, the post is published, with the Subject line as the title and the body as the blog entry itself.

blogging from afar

blog from the toolbar

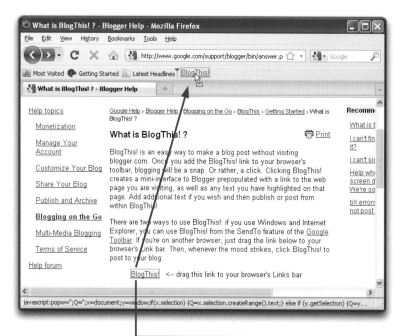

Add a BlogThis! button to your toolbar by first going to the What is BlogThis! page (go to help.blogger.com and search for BlogThis!). Then drag the BlogThis! link to your toolbar. (In Internet Explorer, right-click and add it to your Favorites Bar. Then choose View > Toolbars > Favorites Bar to see it.)

1 Next time you're out on the Web and see a page that you want to talk about on your blog, click your new BlogThis! button.

2 When you click the BlogThis! button, a mini Blogger window pops up with the title of the Web page that you're currently looking at and a link to it in the blog entry box.

3 If you have multiple blogs, choose the one you want to post to.

4 Edit the existing text and/or add your own.

5 When you're ready, click PUBLISH POST (or SAVE AS DRAFT).

The new entry is published in your blog.

extra bits

blog via SMS p. 87

- Not all carriers support go@blogger.com. Another option is to set up a special email address as described in the next section, "set up email blogging" on page 90.

- On the iPhone, sending an SMS or MMS costs extra (unless you have a Messaging plan), but email is included in the base fee. Just saying.

- There are a number of apps in the iTunes Store that let you blog from your iPhone. One of them, BlogPress, lets you post multiple photos with your blog posts, all from your phone. (You can't yet send multiple photos via email with the Mail program on the iPhone.)

set up email blogging p. 90

- If you're the kind of person who gets lots of ideas for your blog on the road, you could choose the Save emails as draft posts option and then email yourself ideas.

blog via email p. 91

- If your email host automatically adds an ad or other extra info to the end of your email, you can keep this from appearing in your blog by typing #end at the desired endpoint of your blog entry.

- Of course, you don't have to include photos. You can send text-only emails too.

- In the illustrations, I use a phone to send the email, but you could conceivably use your desktop computer's email program as well. Although at that point, it's probably easier to use Blogger itself.

blog from the toolbar p. 92

- If you have highlighted text on the Web page when you click the BlogThis! button, the text will be quoted in the BlogThis! window.

- Of course, you don't have to write about the page you're currently visiting. Perhaps it just made you remember something else that you wanted to blog about. In that case, erase the link data and the title and start from scratch.

- Internet Explorer has a hard time with the BlogThis! window because it is reluctant to allow pop-up windows. You might have a better time using the Send To feature on the Google Bar.

7. telling others about yourself

In order to begin using Blogger, you created an account with a user name and password, and a display name. This information is associated with any blog that you create. If you like, you can offer more information about yourself to the people who read your blog. This information is called your Blogger profile.

Of course, how much you tell is completely up to you. You can remain anonymous, or you can give your real name, your location, a description of yourself, your birthdate, and more. Or you can find some compromise between the two extremes. In addition, detailing your interests, favorite books, music, and movies can help you find other bloggers with similar interests.

All the information you choose to share is displayed on your Blogger profile page. You can also have a subset of your profile appear right on your blog along with a link to the full profile page. Either way, the amount of information you share is always up to you.

the About Me gadget

Before you ever edit your profile, Blogger creates a default About Me section— generally in a sidebar in your blog—and populates it with your Display Name and a link to your complete profile.

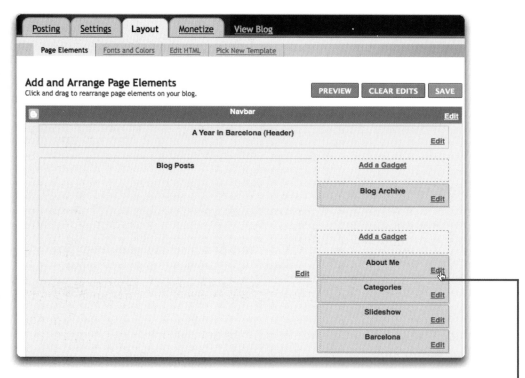

1 You can customize the About Me by going to Layout | Page Elements and clicking the Edit button in the About Me gadget.

2 Edit the text in the Title field to define the header in the sidebar. Blogger uses "About Me" by default.

3 Leave the box checked next to Share my profile if you want to display the About Me section at all.

4 Check (or uncheck) the Show on this blog option next to About Me to display (or hide) your Name and Description (if any) in the About Me gadget in the sidebar. The Description is a great way to describe who you are to your readers.

5 Check (or uncheck) Show on this blog next to Location to display (or hide) your City/Town, Region/State and Country/Territory in the About Me. Enter the info in each location box, as desired.

6 Click Save when you're done.

The Display Name, Location, and Description are now shown in the About Me gadget.

telling others about yourself

view your profile

Your visitors can click the View my complete profile link in the About Me section of your blog to find out more about you. You can click View Profile from the Dashboard.

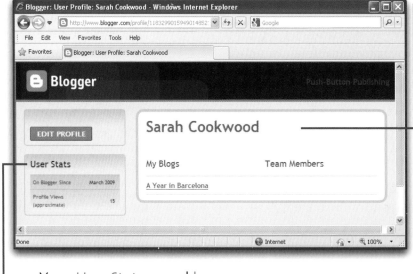

By default, your user profile is publicly available on the Internet. It shows your Display Name, which you chose back on page 3, a list of your blogs, the blog authors that belong to each blog (see page 123), and your User Stats.

Your User Stats reveal how long you've been blogging and approximately how many times your profile has been viewed.

edit your profile

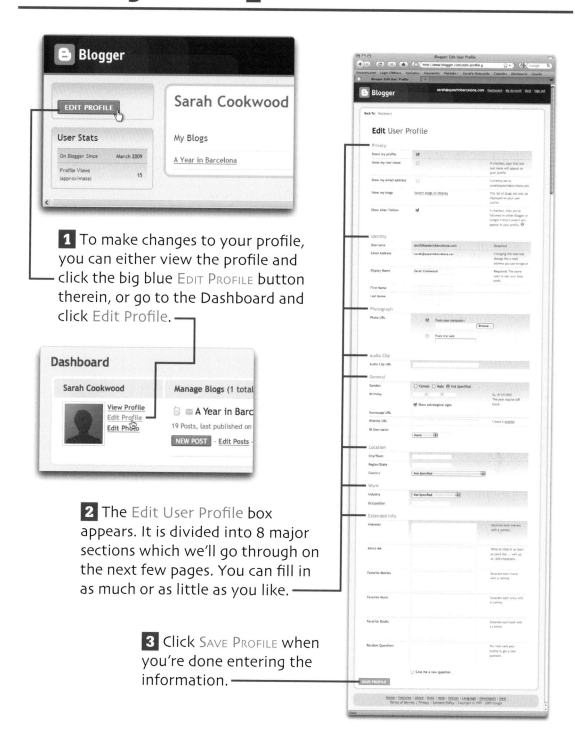

1 To make changes to your profile, you can either view the profile and click the big blue Edit Profile button therein, or go to the Dashboard and click Edit Profile.

2 The Edit User Profile box appears. It is divided into 8 major sections which we'll go through on the next few pages. You can fill in as much or as little as you like.

3 Click Save Profile when you're done entering the information.

edit privacy settings

The first section at the top of the Edit User Profile page is the Privacy settings.

1 Decide if you want to share your profile at all. If you uncheck this box, visitors who try to see your profile will see a message that the profile is not available.

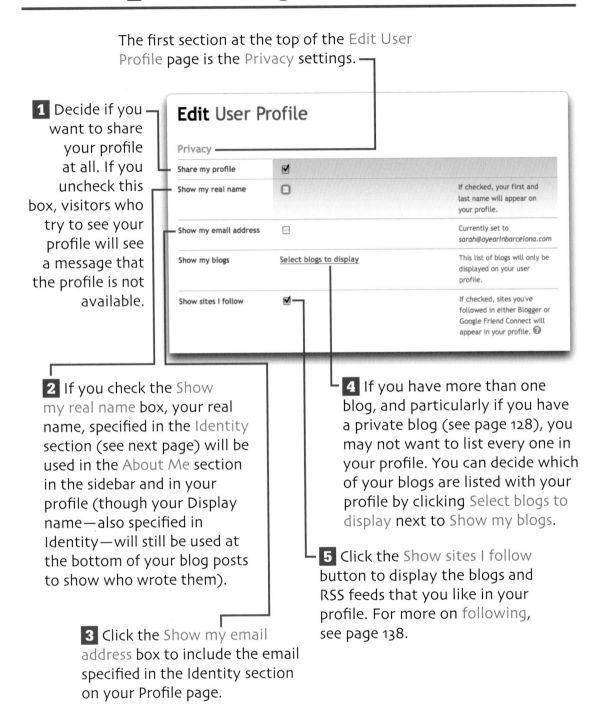

Edit User Profile

Privacy

Share my profile ☑

Show my real name ☐   If checked, your first and last name will appear on your profile.

Show my email address ☐   Currently set to sarah@ayearinbarcelona.com

Show my blogs   Select blogs to display   This list of blogs will only be displayed on your user profile.

Show sites I follow ☑   If checked, sites you've followed in either Blogger or Google Friend Connect will appear in your profile. ❷

2 If you check the Show my real name box, your real name, specified in the Identity section (see next page) will be used in the About Me section in the sidebar and in your profile (though your Display name—also specified in Identity—will still be used at the bottom of your blog posts to show who wrote them).

4 If you have more than one blog, and particularly if you have a private blog (see page 128), you may not want to list every one in your profile. You can decide which of your blogs are listed with your profile by clicking Select blogs to display next to Show my blogs.

5 Click the Show sites I follow button to display the blogs and RSS feeds that you like in your profile. For more on following, see page 138.

3 Click the Show my email address box to include the email specified in the Identity section on your Profile page.

telling others about yourself

edit identity settings

You chose your Username when you created your account (back on page 3). This is the name that is unique to your Blogger account, and that you must use to log in to Google/Blogger.

The email that you specify in the Email Address box is displayed on your Profile when you check the appropriate box in the Privacy section (see previous page). It does not have to match your Username and has nothing to do with logging in.

Identity

Username	sarah@ayearinbarcelona.com	Required
Email Address	sarah@ayearinbarcelona.cor	Changing this does not change the e-mail address you use to sign-in
Display Name	Sarah Cookwood	Required: The name used to sign your blog posts.
First Name	Liz	
Last Name	Castro	

Your Display Name is always used to sign your blog posts. It might be a nickname, or it might be your real name.

a bit crazy... just enough to justify the *seny i rauxa* I keep hearing so much about (*saneness and craziness*: the definition of a Catalan).

Posted by Sarah Cookwood at 6/18/2009 06:18:00 PM   💬 0 comments
Labels: barcelona, holidays

About Me

Liz Castro

👤 **View my complete profile**

The First Name and Last Name fields are for your real name. They are not filled out during the account setup process; you must edit your profile in order to include them. Your real name will appear on your blog in the About Me section (and in your profile) only if you have checked Show my real name on page 100.

add photo to profile

The next section on the Edit Profile page is for adding a photograph. You can also jump here directly by clicking Edit Photo on your Dashboard.

To upload a photo from your computer, click the Browse button and then choose the desired photo. It will be uploaded to your Picasa Web account. Or type the URL of a photo already out on the Web in the From the web box.

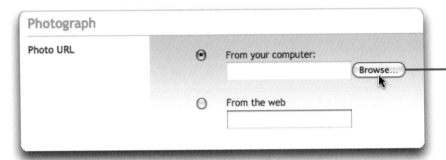

Once you save changes, a thumbnail of the photo appears in the profile. Visitors can see the full size image by clicking View Full Size below the photo.

The photo will also appear in the About Me section of your sidebar.

telling others about yourself

add audio to profile

You can offer your visitors an audio description of yourself on your profile by typing the URL of the audio file in the Audio Clip URL box.

There is no Browse button, which means that Blogger won't host it for you (that is, it has to already be on the Web somewhere). I haven't yet found a format it doesn't support.

Once you save the changes to the profile, a little play button will appear next to the clip so you can preview it.

When visitors view your profile, they'll see a link to the Audio Clip with a little play button next to it. Clicking either the link or the button will play the clip.

add general info

Add the URL of your web site's home page, your Wishlist and/or your IM Username in order to create links to them from your profile.

You can add your Gender or Birthday to your profile. Click Show astrological signs to have Blogger calculate and display your Astrological and Chinese Zodiac Animal signs on your profile.

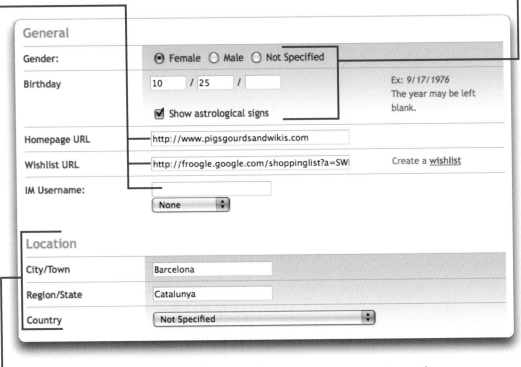

You've already seen how to enter your Location information in the About Me gadget. You can also edit your City/Town, Region/State, and/or Country here, in the Location area of the Edit Profile box.

add searchable bits

The Work, Interests, Favorite Movies, Favorite Music, and Favorite Books sections not only let you tell about yourself but, because the entries are fed into a searchable database, they also let you find other bloggers with similar talents and interests.

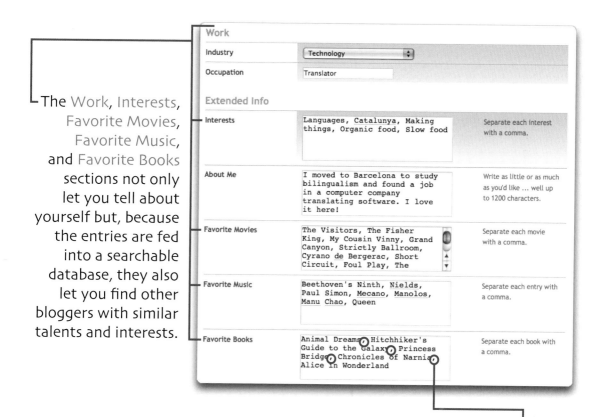

Be sure to separate each discrete occupation, interest, movie, music/musician, or book by a comma (,). Don't add commas within an individual item's words and don't combine similar but distinct items. For example, if you write knitting, writing and reading books, you'll only be found by others who wrote knitting or who wrote writing and reading books. If you write knitting, writing, reading, you'll find others who entered any one of these three terms.

search other profiles

When you go to view your profile, you'll see your Industry, Occupation, Location, Interests, Favorite Movies, Favorite Music, and Favorite Books, converted into search links.

Click one of the links to search for other bloggers with the same interest.

telling others about yourself

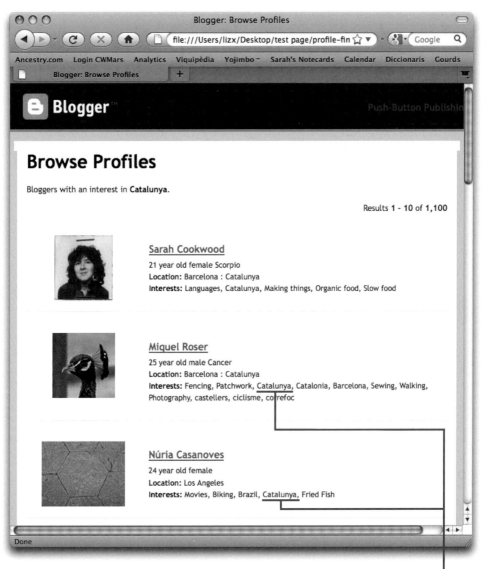

The profiles of other bloggers who have listed the same interest are displayed.

extra bits

the About Me gadget p. 96

- For more information about working with gadgets and page elements, see Chapter 4.

- The Share my profile checkbox also appears in the Privacy section of the main Edit Profile page (see page 100).

- Honestly, it seems weird to me that Blogger lets you control whether or not to share your profile here in the About Me gadget. Letting you control whether or not to show your Name/Description and Location makes more sense. If you have more than one blog, you might want to show these elements on one blog, but not another.

- You can also remove the About Me gadget altogether by clicking the Remove button in the bottom left corner of the dialog box. This way the profile information will not appear in the sidebar of your blog. This will not, however, remove the information from your profile.

- The Description about yourself is your first chance to tell your visitors about yourself and why they should want to read your blog. Use it wisely. You're limited to 1,200 characters.

- The information in the Name field comes from the Display Name that you chose back on page 3, unless you have specified your real First Name and Last Name as described on page 101, and checked the Show my real name box in the Privacy section, in which case it uses those. If you change the value of the Name field in the About Me gadget, Blogger will automatically update the information in the Display Name box and uncheck the Show my real name box in the Identity section of the Edit Profile area (described on page 101).

- Note that the box that appears when you edit your About Me gadget is called Edit Profile. The information that you change here is a subset of the information you can set on your Profile, as we'll see on page 99.

edit your profile p. 99

- Note that you already edited parts of your profile when you adjusted the About Me gadget.

edit privacy settings p. 100

- Of course, if you decide not to share your profile, you might as well skip the rest of this chapter, as it describes how to add information to your profile.

- Unfortunately, if you display your email in your profile, Blogger doesn't protect it from spambots, who go around collecting email addresses from web sites in order to bombard them with stupid spam messages.

edit identity settings p. 101

- Blogger sometimes refers to your Display Name as a Nickname in its online documentation.

- If you have specified both a Display Name and a real First Name and Last Name, the real name is what is used for the About Me section and in the title of your profile. In contrast, the Display Name is always used to show the author of a post. If you don't give your real name, the Display Name is used everywhere.

- When you save changes to your profile, the profile itself is updated immediately. You used to have to republish your blog, but it's not necessary anymore.

add photo to profile p. 102

- If you want visitors to be able to see a large size image (when they click View Full Size), upload a larger image. Blogger will handle the downsizing.

add audio to profile p. 103

- You can use CuteFTP or Fetch to upload the audio file to your own server (most ISPs offer limited amounts of space where you can put things), or choose a file that's already online.

add general info p. 104

- If you prefer, you can enter your birthdate with no year. (But then, Blogger won't be able to calculate your Chinese Zodiac Animal.)

- If you edit the City/Town, Region/State, or Country fields, they will automatically be updated in the About Me gadget. (And if you change them there, they'll be updated here.) Personally, I find it confusing to be able to change them in different places.

- A wishlist is a list of items that you would like to buy—or have others buy for you. You can create wishlists on Amazon or Google Shopping and then add the link here.

extra bits

add searchable bits p. 105

- In earlier versions of Blogger, your Occupation and Location information did not turn into links. Now they do. This makes it easy to find other bloggers with the same job, or from the same place.

search other profiles p. 106

- You'll get one link for each comma-delimited interest. For example, note that Cyrano de Bergerac is one link, not three.
- Currently, this is the only way to search or browse other people's profiles.

telling others about yourself

8. getting others to contribute

Writing a blog can sometimes feel like sending your thoughts out into the ether on a one-way ticket. If you'd like to know what other people thought of your blog, you might want to consider letting them add comments or backlinks to your posts. In this chapter, you'll learn how to control who can leave comments, how to delete comments you don't like, and how to hide comments on one post or on all the posts in a blog. In addition, you'll see how to display and create backlinks.

Of course, comments and backlinks are only a reaction to what you've written in your posts. If you'd like others to help write the blog entries themselves, you can add blog authors to your blog in order to let them create their own entries.

leave/view comments

Unfortunately, they only work with non-grounded flat plugs that have the same size flat prong on either side (as opposed to grounded flat plugs that have one side slightly wider and fatter than the other). After many tries, I finally found a guy who said, "those don't exist, but I can make it for you." And he got out a file and expanded one side so that it fit. I'm not sure if it was grounded, but it did the trick.

Posted by Sarah Cookwood at 9/09/2009 05:09:00 PM 🖂 0 comments

1 At the bottom of each blog entry, by default, you'll see a link that shows how many comments have been received so far. Click it.

fit. I'm not sure if it was grounded, but it did the trick.

Posted by Sarah Cookwood at 9/09/2009 05:09:00 PM 🖂

0 comments:

Post a Comment

> Wow, that is so true. It's funny how Catalans can sometimes be so rigid: "this is the way things are done", and sometimes so flexible: "what, need a new bit, I'll grind you one!"

Comment as: [Google Account ⬦]

(Post Comment) (Preview)

2 You'll jump to the post page for that entry. A post page is one that displays a single blog post. The existing comments and the Post a Comment box are displayed at the bottom. Type your comment in the box.

Comment as: [Select profile... ⬦]
(Post Comme
    Select profile...
    Google Account
    LiveJournal
    WordPress
    TypePad
    AIM
    OpenID

4 Click the Preview button to see what your comment will look like before it is published.

3 By default, only registered visitors who have some kind of OpenID compatible account (including Google, AIM, TypePad, and Wordpress) can add comments to your blog. Choose the type of account you have in the Comment as: pop-up menu.

Sign in to Blogger with your
Google Account

Email: [louise@cookwood.co]
Password: [••••••••]
☐ Stay signed in
(Sign in)

Forgot your password?

Don't have a Google Account?
Create an account now

5 You'll be asked to sign in to the chosen OpenID account.

getting others to contribute

6 Blogger will show you a preview of your comment. Click Edit if you want to change anything.

7 Type the Word verification word to prove that you're a human, and not an automated computer program bent on filling the blog with irrelevant notes full of advertising—known as comment spam. (This task is hard for computers but easy for humans.)

8 Once you're satisfied with your comment, click Post Comment. You'll be returned to the post page, which now displays your comment.

As long as you're signed in, you'll see the garbage can icon, which lets you delete your own comments.

9 Click the Subscribe by email link if you want all the subsequent comments to this post to be sent to your email account (so you can continue the conversation).

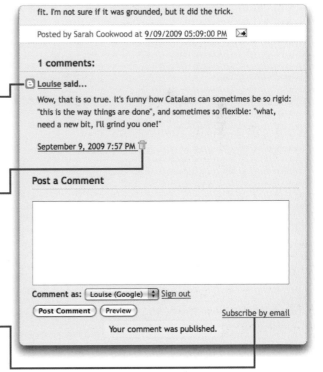

allow anonymity

There are various schools of thoughts about comments. On the one hand, it's nice to get feedback and have a conversation about the topics you're discussing. On the other hand, you probably want to exercise some amount of control over what others write on your blog. Blogger gives you a fair bit of flexibility to choose where you stand on the Settings | Comments page.

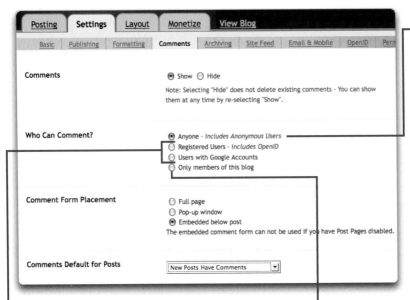

1 To let anyone leave comments on your blog—without necessarily having to sign in—choose Anyone under Who Can Comment? This is likely to get you the most amount of comments.

One way to help ensure that your commenters are legitimate is to require that they be Registered Users (with some kind of OpenID compatible account like Google, AIM, Wordpress or TypePad) or that they be Users with Google Accounts before commenting.

Finally, to keep the tightest control, you can restrict commenting to Only members of this blog (see page 123 for more on blog authors).

2 Click SAVE SETTINGS at the bottom of the page to complete the process.

require humans

You may or may not agree with me that it is OK for folks to post anonymously, but if you do, it's absolutely essential to require that only humans—and no spam spewing robots—be allowed to post.

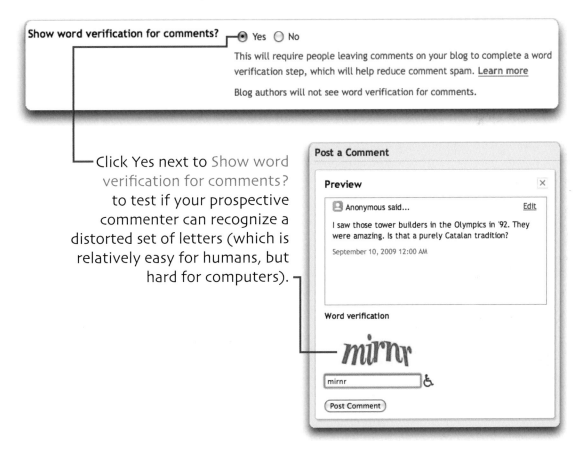

Show word verification for comments? — ⦿ Yes ○ No

This will require people leaving comments on your blog to complete a word verification step, which will help reduce comment spam. **Learn more**

Blog authors will not see word verification for comments.

Click Yes next to Show word verification for comments? to test if your prospective commenter can recognize a distorted set of letters (which is relatively easy for humans, but hard for computers).

Post a Comment

Preview ✕

👤 Anonymous said... Edit

I saw those tower builders in the Olympics in '92. They were amazing. Is that a purely Catalan tradition?

September 10, 2009 12:00 AM

Word verification

mirnr

mirnr &

(Post Comment)

moderate comments

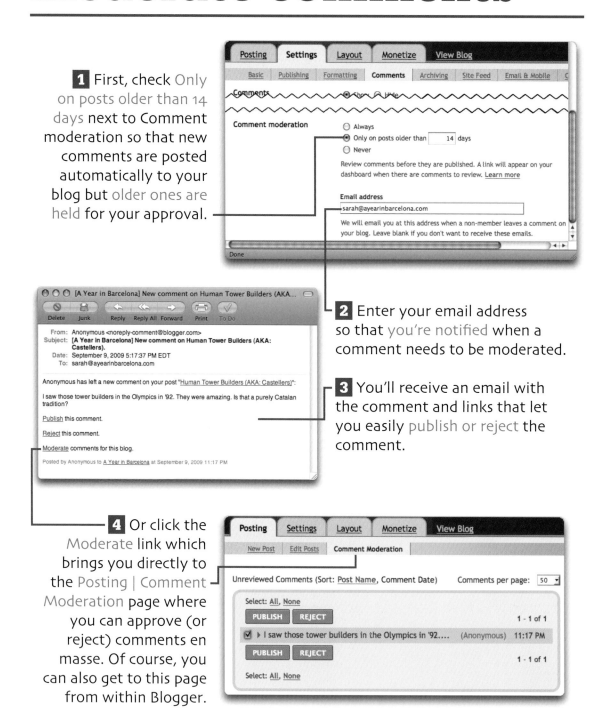

1 First, check Only on posts older than 14 days next to Comment moderation so that new comments are posted automatically to your blog but older ones are held for your approval.

2 Enter your email address so that you're notified when a comment needs to be moderated.

3 You'll receive an email with the comment and links that let you easily publish or reject the comment.

4 Or click the Moderate link which brings you directly to the Posting | Comment Moderation page where you can approve (or reject) comments en masse. Of course, you can also get to this page from within Blogger.

getting others to contribute

get notified

If you've followed the instructions up to this point, you've allowed visitors to comment anonymously (page 114) and you've allowed comments to be posted automatically within 14 days of the post being published (page 116). Both of those actions will allow a certain amount of spam to get through. You want to make sure that you are the first to know it so you can respond immediately. To do so, have Blogger email you each time someone comments on your blog.

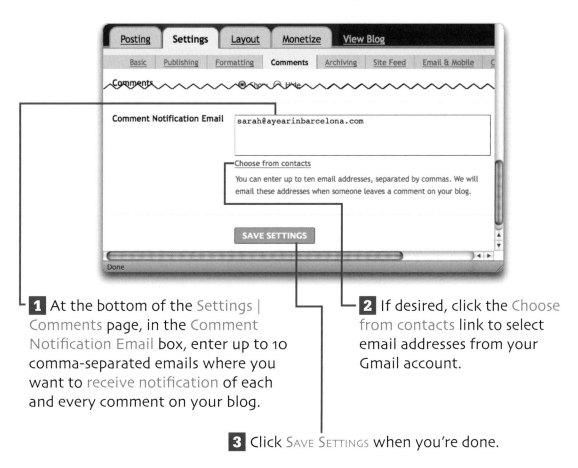

1 At the bottom of the Settings | Comments page, in the Comment Notification Email box, enter up to 10 comma-separated emails where you want to receive notification of each and every comment on your blog.

2 If desired, click the Choose from contacts link to select email addresses from your Gmail account.

3 Click SAVE SETTINGS when you're done.

delete comments

1 You must be signed in to your Blogger account in order to delete unwanted comments.

2 Click the garbage can under the comment that you wish to delete.

1 comments:

Anonymous said...

Get your Human Tower supplies at http://www.HumanTowersRus.com. Cumberbunds, red shirts, helmets, white pants, foot cream. You name it, we've got your human tower equipment!

September 10, 2009 6:34 PM

3 Click DELETE COMMENT to remove the comment from your post.

4 Check Remove forever? to leave no traces of the comment behind.

If you don't check Remove forever (it should really be called Remove completely) the commenter's name and a notice that the comment has been removed remains on the blog.

1 comments:

Anonymous said...

This post has been removed by a blog administrator.

September 10, 2009 6:34 PM

5 Click the garbage icon again for a second chance to remove the comment completely.

getting others to contribute

stop comments

1 If you'd like to stop people from commenting on one particular post, click the Edit button next to the desired post on the Posting | Edit Posts page.

2 On the Posting | Edit Posts page, underneath the body of the post, click the triangle next to Post Options to reveal the choices.

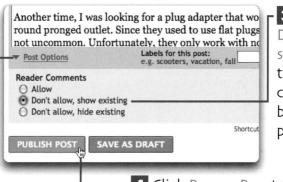

3 Then click Don't allow, show existing so that the current comments remain but no more can be posted.

4 Click PUBLISH POST to save the changes.

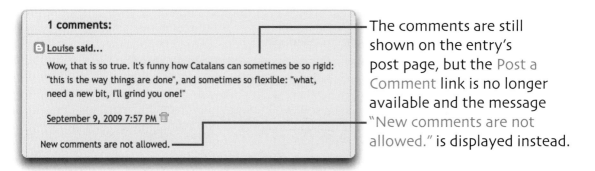

The comments are still shown on the entry's post page, but the Post a Comment link is no longer available and the message "New comments are not allowed." is displayed instead.

hide comments

1 If you want to not only stop people from making new comments but also hide any comments that have already been posted to an individual post, go to that post's Posting | Edit Post page and click Don't allow, hide existing in the Post Options area.

2 Then click PUBLISH POST to save the changes.

1 If you want to hide all of the comments on all of the posts in a blog, go to Settings | Comments and click Hide next to Comments.

2 Then click SAVE SETTINGS at the bottom of the page (not shown).

getting others to contribute

display backlinks

A backlink shows a link from an external site that points to your blog. It can give you an idea who's talking about what you're posting.

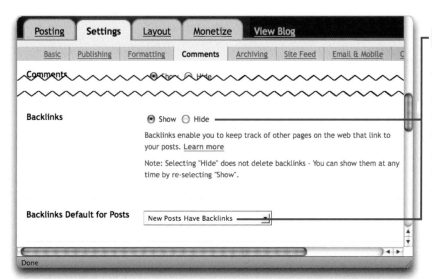

1 By default, Blogger is set up to show backlinks and to allow them on new posts. You can check to make sure in the middle of the Settings | Comments page.

2 However, allowing backlinks as shown above is not enough. Way back in Chapter 4 on page 58, we talked about the Configure Blog Posts box, which comes up when you click the Edit link in the Blog Posts area on the Layout | Page Elements page. To display backlinks, you have to check the Links to this post box (and feel free to change the link text if you like).

3 Then click Save at the bottom of the box (not shown).

create a backlink

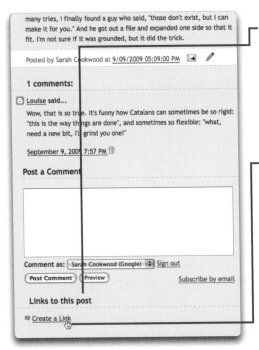

Once you have displayed backlinks as described on the preceding page, a Links to this post area will appear at the bottom of the blog entry's post page. Any links from other sites to this page (that is, backlinks) will be listed here.

1 If a visitor wants to create a link to your blog on their blog, they can click the Create a Link link in the Links to this post section. This is just like using Blog This! (see page 92): a pop-up window appears containing a link to the current page, and the visitor is invited to log in and post a blog entry to their own blog about your blog post.

2 After a few minutes, the new link to your post will appear in the Links to this post area of the page.

Links to this post

▶ Pigs, Gourds, and Wikis: A Year in Barcelona: Hardware Stores par ...
🖉 Create a Link

3 Click the triangle next to the link's title to see the first few lines of text on the linking page, and information about who posted the link.

Links to this post

▼ Pigs, Gourds, and Wikis: A Year in Barcelona: Hardware Stores par ...
So, I'm testing backlinks as I update my book on Blogger. If a regular link goes outward to somewhere else, a backlink is a link from another site to your site. It seems like backlinks are activated by default in Blogger.
...

💬 Posted by Liz Castro at September 10, 2009 8:55 PM

getting others to contribute

add a blog author

If you want other people to be able to publish their own blog posts (and not just comments), you can invite them to be one of the blog authors.

1 Start at the Settings | Permissions page, and click the ADD AUTHORS button.

2 Add the new blog author's email in the box that appears.

When you click INVITE, Blogger will send an email to the address(es) that you specify, inviting them to join your blog by following a link in the email.

3 Once Blogger sends out the invitations, you can check their progress on the Settings | Permissions page.

An Open invitation is one that has not yet been accepted by the prospective blog author.

join another's blog

1 The email invitation that Blogger sends out to your prospective members will look like this.

2 It contains a link that your prospective blog author can click to sign into Google/Blogger and join your blog.

3 When your prospective blog author clicks the link in the email invitation, they'll be directed to sign in to their Blogger account, if they haven't already done so, or create a new one if they don't yet have one.

4 Then, they click ACCEPT INVITATION to join the blog.

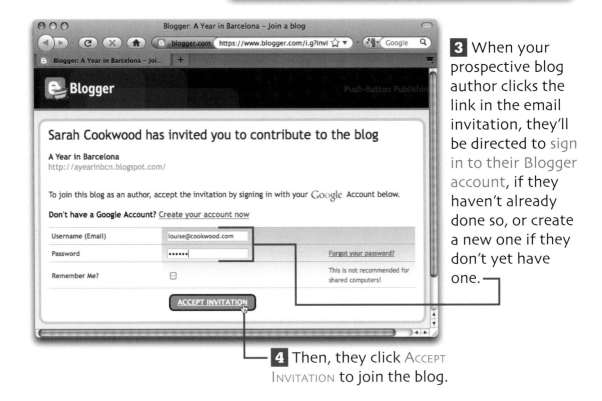

getting others to contribute

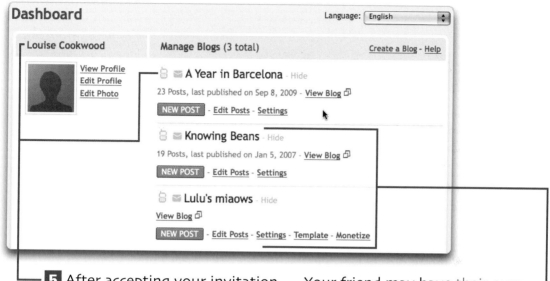

5 After accepting your invitation, your new member will now see your blog on their Dashboard.

Your friend may have their own blogs already; they will continue to be listed on the Dashboard as well.

6 When you log in, you will see the new author added to the Blog Authors list on your Settings | Permissions page. The Blog Authors list shows the member's real name if it is available or the Display Name otherwise.

share responsibility

By default, new blog authors can only add, edit, or delete their own posts. They can't edit or delete other people's posts, nor change any of the blog's settings. Indeed, the Layout and Monetize links for your blog are not even available in your helpers' Dashboards.

If you want to give a blog author the power to change the blog's settings and to edit or delete posts written by any author (including you), click the grant admin privileges link next to their name on the Settings | Permissions page.

getting others to contribute

remove an author

If you want to remove an author from your blog, you'll have to go to the Settings | Permissions page and click the remove link next to their name. Their permissions are removed but their blog entries are not. You can delete them manually by going to the Posting | Edit Posts page.

restrict access

1 Go to the bottom of the Settings | Permissions page where you control who can read your blog.

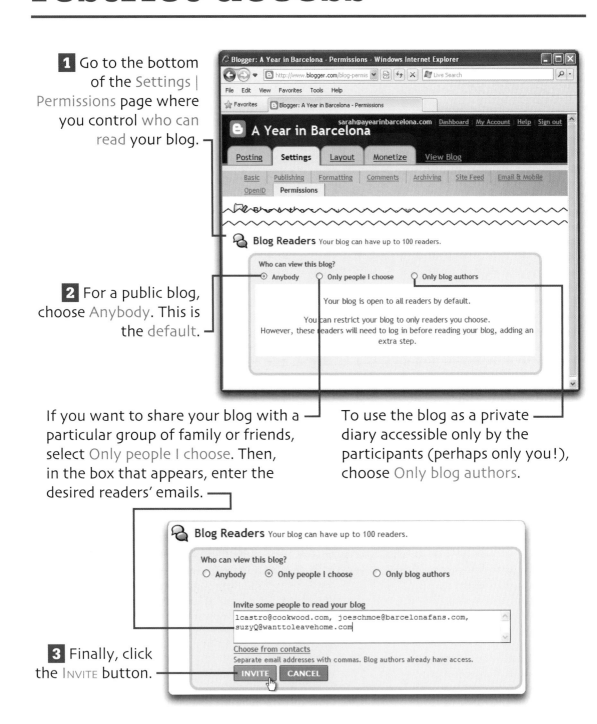

2 For a public blog, choose Anybody. This is the default.

If you want to share your blog with a particular group of family or friends, select Only people I choose. Then, in the box that appears, enter the desired readers' emails.

To use the blog as a private diary accessible only by the participants (perhaps only you!), choose Only blog authors.

3 Finally, click the INVITE button.

getting others to contribute

extra bits

leave/view comments p. 112

- Blogger's default settings require visitors to sign in—and thus have a Google/Blogger account—before they can leave comments. While this can help protect your blog from unwelcome comment spam, it can also keep visitors from making legitimate comments. I show you how to accept comments from anyone, even without a Blogger account, on page 114.

- Sometimes, comments don't appear right away, as we'll see on page 116.

allow anonymity p. 114

- It has been my experience that making people register before they comment will significantly reduce the amount of comments received.

require humans p. 115

- Using Word verification is Blogger's default option. Only turn it off if you have other antispam measures set up.

moderate comments p. 116

- Moderated comments are not posted right away. Visitors who post a comment that gets moderated will see this notification:

> Your comment will be visible after approval.

- Blogger will also let you know that you have comments to moderate with a message to that effect on your dashboard:

Click the link to jump to the Posting | Comment Moderation page.

- Unless you have chosen Only blog members on page 128, it's absolutely essential that you moderate your comments. If you don't, you may find your blog filled with unwanted ads and rude commentary. A spammer's favorite ploy is to add links onto an older, but still popular blog post that you're not watching as carefully.

extra bits

- If you have a busy, public blog, it may be better to moderate all comments. To do so, click Always next to Comment moderation. In that case, comments won't be posted until you reject or approve them on the Posting | Comment Moderation page.

delete comments p. 118

- Visitors can also remove their own comments as long as they have signed in with the same Blogger account that they used when posting the comment.

- Nobody besides the commenter and the blog owner will see the garbage can icon.

- The Remove forever? checkbox implies that if you don't check it there might be some way to recover a deleted comment. That's not the case. It's simply badly named. It should be called Remove completely? since when you check it, Blogger leaves no trace of the comment.

- Sometimes bloggers like to leave the remains of a deleted comment to show both that they get a lot of comments and that they are keeping them under control. Me? I delete completely!

stop comments p. 119

- You can let people add comments again at any time by going back to the Posting | Edit Posts page for that entry and clicking Allow under Reader Comments in the Posting Options section.

- If you'd like to not only disallow future comments but also hide any comments that have already been posted, click Don't allow, hide existing. Note that hidden comments are not deleted and will reappear if you choose a different option for Reader Comments.

- Commenting is allowed on new posts by default. Change the default on the Settings | Comments page by choosing New Posts Do Not Have Comments next to Comments Default for Posts.

hide comments p. 120

- Comments are not deleted when you hide them. If you decide you want to show them again, you can click Show on the Settings | Comments page. That also means you can't delete all the comments and start over from scratch. The old comments remain (though you can delete them as described on page 118).

getting others to contribute

display backlinks p. 121

- Backlinks are a great way to see if other people are blogging about what you've blogged. While comments are conversations between individuals about your posts, backlinks are conversations between blogs or web sites about your posts.

create a backlink p. 122

- For more information about using Blog This!, see page 92.

- The Create a Link option is only useful for creating backlinks on Blogger blogs. If someone wants to create a link to your blog from anywhere else—any kind of blog or web site or whatever—they can just do it in the normal way. Blogger will find the link and report it in the backlinks section no matter how it was created.

add a blog author p. 123

- New blog authors will be able to post, edit, and delete their own entries, but won't be able to modify other authors' posts or change the blog's settings.

- If you change your mind about adding a new author, or if you add the wrong email address, you can cancel the invitation by clicking the remove link next to the person's address in the Open Invitations table.

- If an invited author doesn't respond after a while, you can remind them to join by clicking the send again link in the Open Invitations table.

remove an author p. 127

- You can't remove an author's admin privileges unless at least one other author has admin privileges.

- You can change ownership of your blog to another person by adding them as a blog author, making them an Admin as described on page 126, and then removing your own privileges. Note, however, that as soon as you click the revoke admin privileges link next to your own name, you will immediately be locked out of the Settings | Permissions page for that blog. You won't be able to change the blog settings unless and until the other Admin returns the admin privileges to you.

extra bits

- Blogger restricts access to protect-
  ed blogs by requiring blog readers
  to sign in with their Google/Blog-
  ger account when they go to view
  your blog.

- You can use Blogger to organize
  a completely private journal for
  yourself, that no-one else can
  read, by making yourself the sole
  blog author, and restricting access
  to Only blog authors.

- If you create a private blog, be
  sure not to list it in your profile.
  You can adjust which blogs are
  listed by editing your profile and
  clicking the Select blogs to display
  option. For more details, see "edit
  privacy settings" on page 100.

9. getting the word out

Once you start writing, you'll probably want someone to read your blog. You can start by sending out an email with your blog's address to all your friends and relations.

If you want to attract a wider audience, you can take advantage of Blogger's listings and syndicating features, as well as Google's other tools for analyzing Web traffic, all described in this chapter.

list your blog

On every Blogger Dashboard, there is a Reading List with a tab marked Blogs of Note. These are chosen by Blogger's staff.

On the Navigation Bar, you'll find a Next Blog link that brings you to another Blogger blog about the same or a related topic.

Blogger Play displays recently uploaded images from Blogger blogs.

1 If you're OK with Blogger including your blog in Blogs of Note, Next Blog or Blogger Play, choose Yes next to Add your blog to our listings? on the Settings | Basic page.

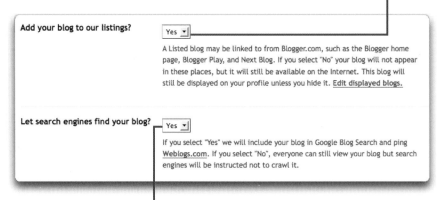

2 If you want your blog included in Google Blog Search, choose Yes next to Let search engines find your blog? If you're creating a private blog, and don't want it indexed, choose No.

email new posts

If you'd like to let someone know each time you post a new entry, add their email to the BlogSend Address field on the Settings | Email & Mobile page. Blogger will send your new posts to up to 10 (comma-separated) email addresses.

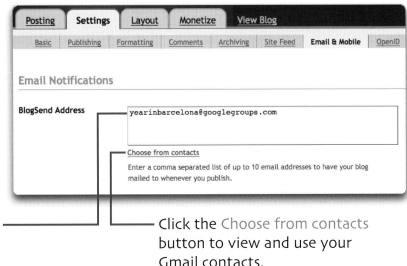

Click the Choose from contacts button to view and use your Gmail contacts.

Better yet, create a mailing list or Google group (start at groups.google.com) for all those who want to know when you've posted a new blog entry. Then put the group's email in the BlogSend Address field above.

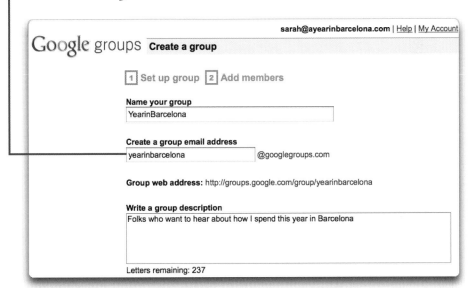

syndicate your blog

Syndicating your blog means making it available to other programs, generally in the form of an RSS feed, in order to make it easy for readers to subscribe and otherwise keep up to date with what you're writing.

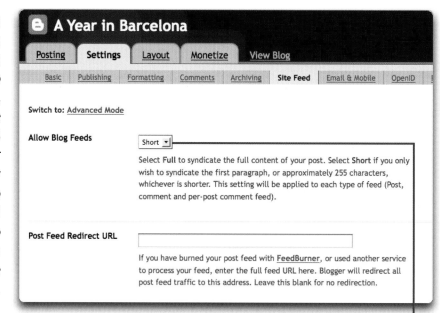

On the Settings | Site Feed page, choose Short next to Descriptions if you want just the first part of your blog entry to be listed in the newsreader. Choose Long if you want the entire entry to appear in the newsreader.

If you publish a site feed as shown above, your visitors can use a newsreader like Google Reader to subscribe to that feed.

add subscription links

Most browsers will give your visitors some way to subscribe to your blog's feed and thus be apprised when you've published a new post. For example, in IE, the RSS feed icon in the Commands toolbar turns orange when a feed is available. Visitors can click the icon to subscribe to the blog.

Another option is to add a Subscription Links gadget to your sidebar. (See page 61 for details on adding gadgets.)

Then your readers can click the options in the Subscribe To area of your sidebar and add your blog to their preferred RSS reader.

encourage followers

A follower is someone who has subscribed to your blog through Blogger. You can encourage followers by displaying your existing followers and making it easy for new people to follow you.

Add the Followers gadget to your blog. (For more on adding gadgets, see page 61.)

Followers (New!)
Displays a list of users who follow your blog
By Blogger

The Followers gadget is inserted in the sidebar. It includes a Follow link which facilitates joining your blog as well as a current list of Followers.

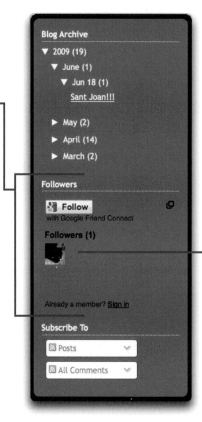

On this brand new blog, we just have a single follower, but as we grow, more people will join, which in turn may encourage even more folks to follow.

getting the word out

follow other blogs

Another way to encourage people to
follow your blog is to follow theirs.

1 If they have a
Followers gadget like
you created on the
previous page, you
can click the Follow
button. Or you can
start from your
Dashboard, by clicking
the Add button at the
bottom of the Reading
List. Either way, you'll
get the Add Blogs to
Follow box.

2 Type or paste the URL of the blog you wish
to follow in the Add from URL box. Or, if you're
already subscribed to blogs via Google Reader,
you can import them as well. Then, click NEXT.

3 Choose to follow a blog publicly, with your name and photo
on their Followers page or gadget, or privately. Then click FOLLOW.
Either way, the followed blog will show up in your Reading List
on your Dashboard (and in your Google Reader account).

share posts

1 One of Blogger's newer features is the Share button on the Navigation bar. You (or your visitors) can click the Share button to share your blog (or a particular post if one is chosen) via Twitter, Facebook, or Google Reader.

2 Once you click the Share button, you can choose the service you wish to use.

3 You are then brought to your account on the chosen service (Twitter, in this example), and the title of your blog, along with its URL and a special tag (?spref=tw) are used as the default sharing text.

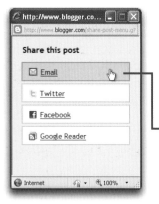

If you click the Share button while viewing an individual blog post, you'll also have the option of emailing that post to a friend or colleague.

let visitors email posts

Another way to make it easy for your visitors to email your posts to their friends, thus publicizing your blog, is to add an Email Post link icon to your blog by choosing Yes from the Show Email Post links? menu on the Settings | Basic page.

The Email Post link icon (in the form of an envelope) appears in the byline of your post. When a visitor clicks it, they are asked for their name and email and the email of their friend. Blogger then emails your post to your visitor's friend.

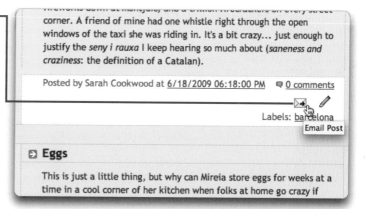

get indexed

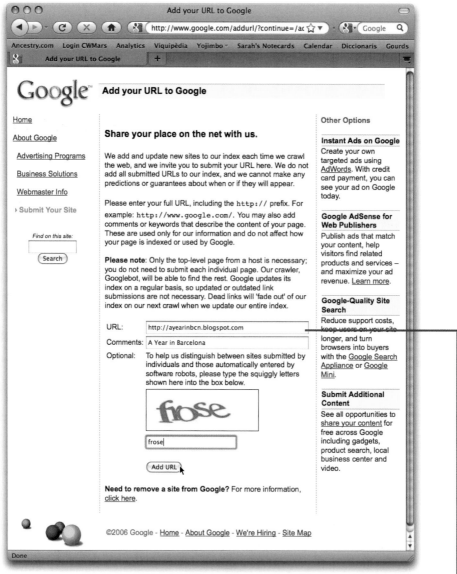

Once your blog is published, you can invite Google to visit and add your blog to its index by sending your URL (Web address) through the Add your URL to Google page at http://www.google.com/addurl.html.

track your visitors

Google Analytics counts the number of visitors to your site. It can tell where folks came from, what search words they used, what they looked at, and when they left. It can help you figure out what you need to get more traffic.

1 Start by pointing your browser at https://www. google.com/analytics/provision/ If you're not already a Google Analytics user, you'll have to click the Sign Up » button.

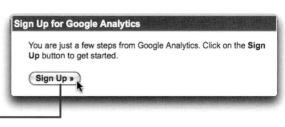

Sign Up for Google Analytics

You are just a few steps from Google Analytics. Click on the **Sign Up** button to get started.

(Sign Up »)

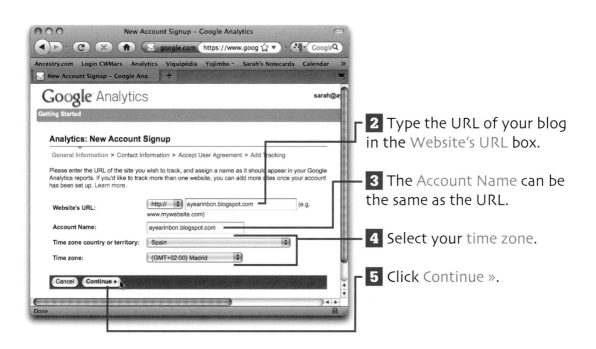

2 Type the URL of your blog in the Website's URL box.

3 The Account Name can be the same as the URL.

4 Select your time zone.

5 Click Continue ».

continued...

getting the word out

track your visitors

6 Continue to fill in your information and accept the Terms of Service. Once you do, Google Analytics will show you the tracking code that you have to add to your blog so that Google can tell what people are doing there.

7 Select and copy the entire block of code from the text box in the middle of the Tracking Instructions page.

8 Then click Finish.

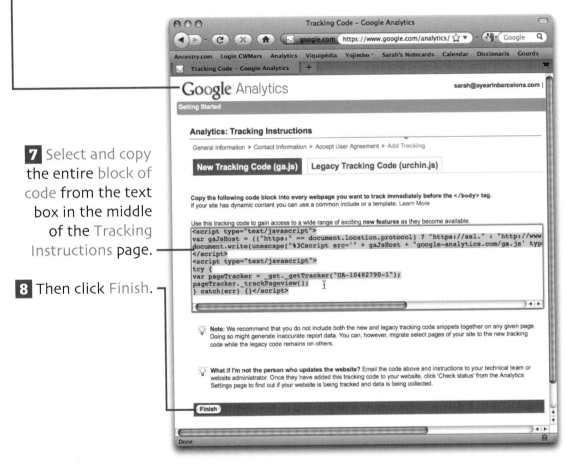

9 Go back to Blogger, and add the HTML/JavaScript gadget to your bottom-most sidebar or footer. (See page 61 for details on adding gadgets.)

HTML/JavaScript
Add third-party functionality or other code to your blog.
By Blogger

Blogger :: A Year in Barcelona :: Configure HTML/JavaScript

http://www.blogger.com/rearrange?blogID=7244475022129073728&secti

Configure HTML/JavaScript ? Help

Title

Content   **b** *i* 💬 66 | Rich Text

```
<script type="text/javascript">
var gaJsHost = (("https:" == document.location.protocol) ?
"https://ssl." : "http://www.");
document.write(unescape("%3Cscript src='" + gaJsHost +
"google-analytics.com/ga.js' type='text/javascript'%3E%3C
/script%3E"));
</script>
<script type="text/javascript">
try {
var pageTracker = _gat._getTracker("UA-10482790-1");
pageTracker._trackPageview();
} catch(err) {}</script>
```

BACK   CANCEL   SAVE

javascript:void(0)

10 Leave the Title box empty, since you want the code to be invisible.

11 Paste the tracking code that you copied in step 6 on the previous page into the Content box.

12 Click SAVE.

Barcelona
→ Barcelona Turisme
→ Generalitat de Catalunya
→ City of Barcelona

Add a Gadget

About Me   Edit

Categories   Edit

Slideshow   Edit

Barcelona   Edit

HTML/JavaScript Edit

13 Drag the new gadget to the bottom of its sidebar or footer.

14 You shouldn't be able to see the new code on your blog, but it's there! (You can View Source to be sure.)

analyze your traffic

Once it's set up, Google Analytics offers a wealth of information about the traffic to and from your blog.

Use the links in the Dashboard sidebar to navigate to the different areas of the site.

Click the links in the Site Usage area to see how many visits your getting, which days or times folks visit, how many pages the view, how quickly they leave, and how many are there for the first time.

Use the Help Resources links to find out more about Google Analytics. There's so much!

Drag your mouse along the Visitors Overview graph to see how many people visited on a given day. Or click the view report link to get all the data.

View the Traffic Sources Overview report to see which sites visitors are coming from. Are they finding you through a search engine? If so, what keywords did they search for? Did someone link to you? If so, who was it and what did they say? Or did they come directly?

getting the word out

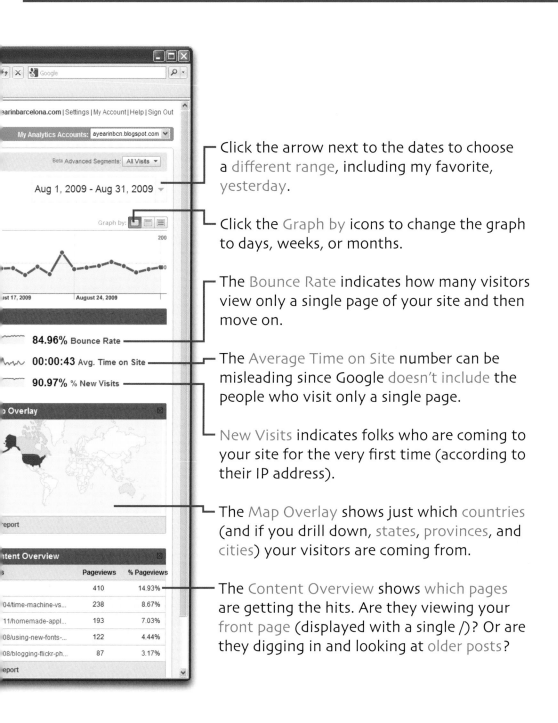

Click the arrow next to the dates to choose a different range, including my favorite, yesterday.

Click the Graph by icons to change the graph to days, weeks, or months.

The Bounce Rate indicates how many visitors view only a single page of your site and then move on.

The Average Time on Site number can be misleading since Google doesn't include the people who visit only a single page.

New Visits indicates folks who are coming to your site for the very first time (according to their IP address).

The Map Overlay shows just which countries (and if you drill down, states, provinces, and cities) your visitors are coming from.

The Content Overview shows which pages are getting the hits. Are they viewing your front page (displayed with a single /)? Or are they digging in and looking at older posts?

extra bits

list your blog p. 134

- Blogger includes your blog in its listings by default. If you'd rather not be included, pick No instead. For more about private blogs, see page 128.

- Of course, agreeing to be listed does not guarantee you will be. The blogs listed in Blogs of Note (http://blogsofnote.blogspot.com) are chosen by the Blogger staff, and the blogs featured in Next Blog and Blogger Play are chosen more or less at random.

- If you check the Let search engines find your blog? box, Blogger will also notify Weblogs.com—a web site written by Dave Winer (a weblogging pioneer) that publishes a list of recently updated blogs—each time you add a post to your blog.

email new posts p. 135

- Google Groups is a simple, free way to create a newsgroup.

- You should be careful about subscribing people to your list without asking them first. Google lets you invite, rather than directly subscribe members if you like.

- Some Web hosts offer free mailing lists as part of their hosting package. Contact yours to see if they do and for details about how to set up a list.

- If you have a team blog (see page 123) you can add your own email to the BlogSend Address to notify yourself if one of the other team members posts an entry.

email new posts p. 135

- If you add more than one email to the BlogSend Address box, be sure to separate each one with a comma.

syndicate your blog p. 136

- Syndicating your blog makes the blog available for visitors to subscribe to, but they have to do the actual subscribing themselves. It's a good idea to provide links to additional information or to particular newsreaders as described on page 137.

- The address for your blog's RSS feed is http://blogname.blogspot.com/feeds/posts/default, where blogname is the name of your blog. You can find the RSS feeds for your comments and specific posts at this URL: http://bit.ly/BloggerFeeds.

getting the word out

- If you publish Short feeds, you may entice your readers to come visit your actual site (increasing your traffic, and perhaps seeing other articles of interest), or conversely, they may simply not read the entire article.

- Feedburner, part of Google, is a service that keeps track of the number of people that subscribe to your blog. It can also tell you if they've clicked through to your site, what reader they're using, and more. Go to feedburner. google.com to sign up.

- If you click the show details link in Google Reader, it shows you how many subscribers the blog has.

add subscription links p. 137
- Blogger publishes its site feeds in both Atom and RSS formats. You can see what the feeds look like at http://bit.ly/BloggerFeeds.

encourage followers p. 138
- Followers is Google's way of subscribing to a blog using its Friend-Connect social networking service, and presumably RSS. Visitors who follow your blog through Blogger will be automatically subscribed through Google Reader as well.

- Blogger adds the Followers gadget to blogs by default. It's not as useful when your blog is new, but once you have a following, the Followers gadget can help attract new followers.

follow other blogs p. 139
- Even if you follow a blog publicly, only your Display Name will be used unless you have given permission to use your real name (as described on page 101).

- Blogs that you follow will also appear automatically in your Google Reader account.

share posts p. 140
- Even if you don't use Blogger's Share button, it's a great idea to announce your posts with Twitter or Facebook.

get indexed p. 142
- There are people who make a living by getting web sites indexed. There are three important techniques: 1. Use the keywords that people will use to search for you throughout your site and in a meaningful way, especially in the title, headers, and first paragraph. 2. Get linked from other sites. 3. Submit your site to Google.

extra bits

track your visitors p. 144

- You can return to the Tracking Code page if you need to find the code again by clicking Edit next to the project on the Overview page, and then Check Status in the upper-right corner of the window.

- Google's Webmaster Tools offers other useful resources for analyzing traffic. See http://bit.ly/WebmasterOrAnalytics for details.

- You can use Google Analytics with any web site, not just a Blogger blog.

- You can track multiple web sites with Google Analytics. To add a new site to your account, go to the bottom of the main Overview window, and click Add Website Profile».

> **Add Website Profile»**
> A profile allows you to track a website and/or create different views of the reporting data using filters. Learn more

- With some of Blogger's templates, including the one used here, when you add an HTML/JavaScript gadget to the footer, you can see an empty frame. If you add the gadget to an area that already has some gadgets like the sidebar, it will be completely invisible.

analyze your traffic p. 146

- I could write a whole book on Google Analytics, maybe even two. I recommend exploring all it has to offer: click all the links, try out the different custom options, see what you find!

- It's a good idea to exclude your own hits from Google Analytics' results. First, find your IP address by googling "what is my IP" and copying the result. Next, from the Analytics' Overview page, click the Edit button next to your Website profile. Click Add Filter+ next to Filters applied to profile. Then type something like "Exclude me" for the Filter Name, choose "Exclude all traffic from an IP address" from the Filter type menu, and paste your IP in the IP address box. Click Save changes to finish. As your ISP periodically changes your IP address, you may have to update this setting.

getting the word out

10. getting paid to blog

The most important element in making your blog profitable is creating interesting content on your web site that someone might want to come and read. Once you've got that piece taken care of, you can work on placing ads on your site that your visitors might find useful enough to click, and by doing so, generate income for you.

Because of the connection between Google and Blogger, Blogger has several tools that facilitate placing Google ads on your blog. If those tools aren't robust enough, you can go directly to the source at Google's AdSense web site and customize the ads to your liking.

In addition, you can add just about any affiliate program's ad codes to an HTML/JavaScript gadget on Blogger in order to include their ads on your blog as well.

about AdSense

AdSense, as Google's web site explains, is part of Google's advertising ecosystem. Here's how it works. First, Google sells space, or "ad units", to companies that want to advertise their products. Ad units currently come in 18 sizes and can be composed of text, images, or video, or some combination thereof. Google then categorizes the ads in terms of content.

Since it makes most sense to advertise a product to folks interested in that product, Google doesn't place its clients' ads randomly. Instead, when you sign up for the AdSense program, Google assesses your site and decides which of its clients' ads are a good match for your content. It then feeds ads to your site that it considers to be of possible interest to your visitors, given the content on your page.

When one of your visitors clicks on a Google AdSense ad, Google gives you a commission.

Because Blogger and AdSense are sister programs under Google's umbrella, there are special tools and shortcuts that make implementing AdSense on Blogger particularly easy. Nevertheless, you can always visit AdSense's web site directly, where you will find additional options not offered through Blogger.

set up AdSense

1 To begin with Google AdSense, click the Monetize link on the Dashboard, or the Monetize tab within your blog.

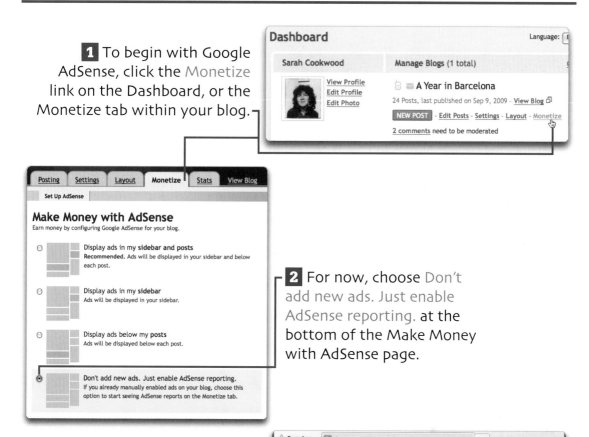

2 For now, choose Don't add new ads. Just enable AdSense reporting. at the bottom of the Make Money with AdSense page.

3 Assuming you don't yet have an account, click the Create a new AdSense account button.

4 Then click NEXT.

5 Fill out all the electronic paperwork until you see that AdSense has been enabled for your blog (not shown).

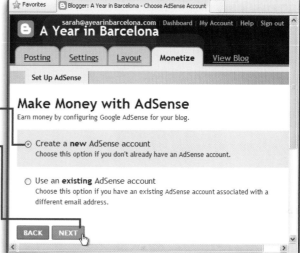

add an AdSense gadget

1 There are two ways to put an ad on your blog. The first and simplest is to add an AdSense gadget. Start by going to the Layout | Page Elements page and clicking Add a Gadget.

2 Choose the AdSense gadget from the list that appears.

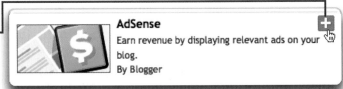

AdSense
Earn revenue by displaying relevant ads on your blog.
By Blogger

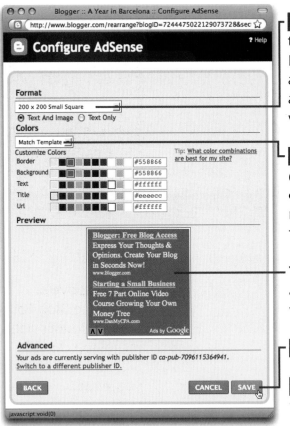

3 Choose an ad size that fits well in the desired location. Most standard Blogger layouts have sidebars that are about 220 pixels wide. The central area ranges from 460 to 480 pixels wide.

4 Choose individual or a set of colors (called a template) for the ad. I like to choose the same colors that I use in my blog design so that the ads aren't too garish and distracting.

You can see a preview of the ad, at actual size, in the lower part of the window.

5 Click SAVE to place the ad.

6 Repeat the process for each ad you want to insert (up to 3 on a page).

getting paid to blog

adjust ad placement

Like any gadget, an AdSense gadget can be moved about to a new location in the Layout | Page Elements page by dragging (see page 54 for details). With the Rounders template, I like putting an AdSense gadget in one of the sidebars by itself.

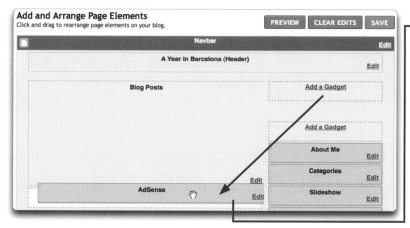

Even though there is no Add a Gadget option above or below the Blog Posts area, that does not mean you can't drag one there after you've added it to a sidebar.

add inline ads

Inline ads appear between one blog post and the next (as opposed to after the last blog post).

1 To place inline ads, revisit the Configure Blog Posts box by clicking the Edit link in the Blog Posts area on the Layout | Page Elements page (see page 58 for details).

2 Click Show Ads Between Posts. (It's the last option in the list.)

3 In the Configure Inline Ads area that now appears, choose how often the ads should appear.

4 Then choose the desired size. For inline ads, I recommend 468 x 60 Banner.

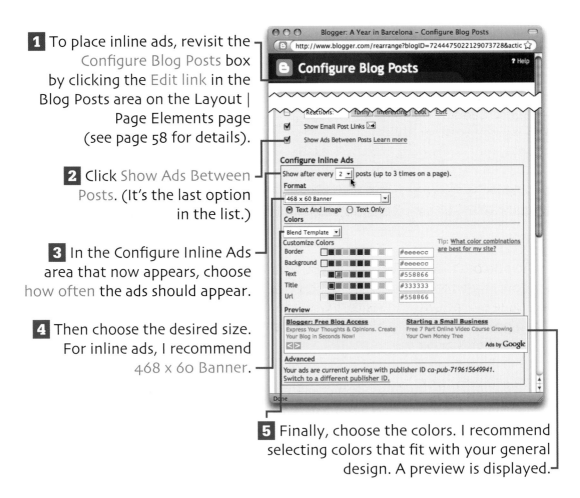

5 Finally, choose the colors. I recommend selecting colors that fit with your general design. A preview is displayed.

getting paid to blog

use the AdSense site

Google's AdSense site lets you customize your ads, create channels for tracking particular sites or ads, create search boxes, insert ads in feeds, and more.

1 Start at http://www.google.com/adsense.

2 Click AdSense for Content. Instead of using the automated AdSense gadget, on the next few pages, we'll use AdSense's site to customize many features for the same kind of ad.

3 Click CONTINUE at the bottom of the window to go to the next page of options. Then go to the next page in this book.

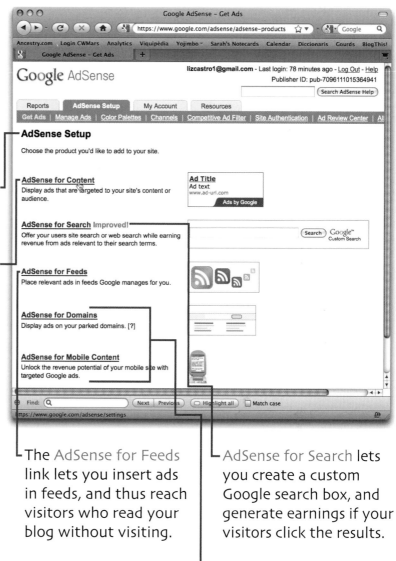

The AdSense for Feeds link lets you insert ads in feeds, and thus reach visitors who read your blog without visiting.

AdSense for Search lets you create a custom Google search box, and generate earnings if your visitors click the results.

AdSense for Domains lets you place ads on domains you have bought but don't yet use, while AdSense for Mobile Content is designed specifically for sites accessed with a mobile device, like a phone.

ad units vs. link units

The first thing you have to choose after clicking AdSense for Content on the main AdSense page is whether or not you want to create an ad unit or a link unit.

4 Choose Ad unit to allow images and video along with text, as well as more descriptive text-only ads.

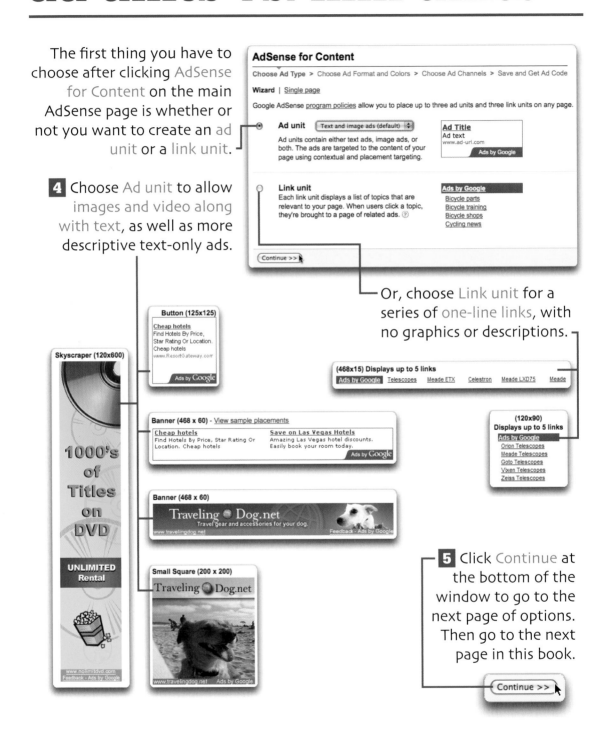

AdSense for Content

Choose Ad Type > Choose Ad Format and Colors > Choose Ad Channels > Save and Get Ad Code

Wizard | Single page

Google AdSense program policies allow you to place up to three ad units and three link units on any page.

Ad unit [Text and image ads (default)]
Ad units contain either text ads, image ads, or both. The ads are targeted to the content of your page using contextual and placement targeting.

Ad Title
Ad text
www.ad-url.com
Ads by Google

Link unit
Each link unit displays a list of topics that are relevant to your page. When users click a topic, they're brought to a page of related ads. ⑦

Ads by Google
Bicycle parts
Bicycle training
Bicycle shops
Cycling news

Continue >>

Or, choose Link unit for a series of one-line links, with no graphics or descriptions.

Skyscraper (120x600)
1000's of Titles on DVD
UNLIMITED Rental
www.nolimitdvd.com
Feedback - Ads by Google

Button (125x125)
Cheap hotels
Find Hotels By Price, Star Rating Or Location. Cheap hotels
www.ResortGateway.com
Ads by Google

(468x15) Displays up to 5 links
Ads by Google Telescopes Meade ETX Celestron Meade LXD75 Meade

Banner (468 x 60) - View sample placements
Cheap hotels
Find Hotels By Price, Star Rating Or Location. Cheap hotels
Save on Las Vegas Hotels
Amazing Las Vegas hotel discounts. Easily book your room today.
Ads by Google

(120x90)
Displays up to 5 links
Ads by Google
Orion Telescopes
Meade Telescopes
Goto Telescopes
Vixen Telescopes
Zeiss Telescopes

Banner (468 x 60)
Traveling ● Dog.net
Travel gear and accessories for your dog.
www.travelingdog.net
Feedback - Ads by Google

Small Square (200 x 200)
Traveling ● Dog.net
www.travelingdog.net Ads by Google

5 Click Continue at the bottom of the window to go to the next page of options. Then go to the next page in this book.

Continue >>

format and colors

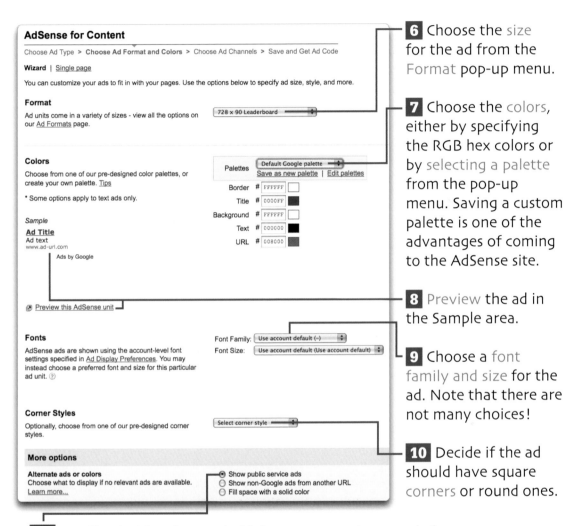

6 Choose the size for the ad from the Format pop-up menu.

7 Choose the colors, either by specifying the RGB hex colors or by selecting a palette from the pop-up menu. Saving a custom palette is one of the advantages of coming to the AdSense site.

8 Preview the ad in the Sample area.

9 Choose a font family and size for the ad. Note that there are not many choices!

10 Decide if the ad should have square corners or round ones.

11 Finally, decide what to do if there are no relevant ads for your site. The default is for Google to show public service ads, but you can also choose to enter a URL for an image or static ad of your choosing, or to fill the ad space with a solid color.

12 Click Continue at the bottom of the window to go to the next page of options. Then go to the next page in this book.

track ads with channels

Think of an AdSense channel as the conduit by which traffic runs through your site to the advertiser. You can get earnings reports broken down by channel in order to see how your ads are working on a particular domain or subdomain (through a URL channel), or in a particular location (through a custom channel).

13 On the third page of creating your AdSense for Content ad, click Add new channel (or click add>> next to an existing custom channel).

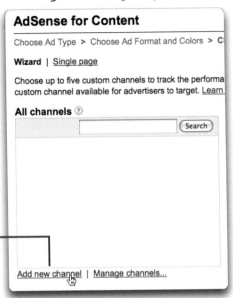

AdSense for Content

Choose Ad Type > Choose Ad Format and Colors > C

Wizard | Single page

Choose up to five custom channels to track the performa custom channel available for advertisers to target. Learn

All channels ⑦

[   ] (Search)

Add new channel | Manage channels...

The page at https://www.google.com says:

Please enter a name for your new channel

[green sidebar]

(Cancel)　(OK)

14 Give the channel a name that identifies its location or the kind of ad it will contain.

15 Click Continue at the bottom of the window to go to the next page of options. Then go to the next page in this book.

(Continue >>)

name your ad

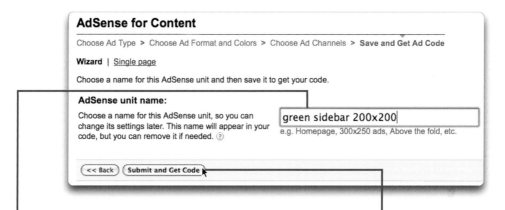

AdSense for Content

Choose Ad Type > Choose Ad Format and Colors > Choose Ad Channels > **Save and Get Ad Code**

Wizard | Single page

Choose a name for this AdSense unit and then save it to get your code.

AdSense unit name:

Choose a name for this AdSense unit, so you can change its settings later. This name will appear in your code, but you can remove it if needed. ⑦

green sidebar 200x200

e.g. Homepage, 300x250 ads, Above the fold, etc.

(<< Back) (Submit and Get Code)

16 Another advantage of creating your ad on the AdSense site is that you can name the collection of settings that you used to make the ad and then use it again in some other situation.

17 Click Submit and Get Code. On the next page, you'll see how to add the code to your blog.

place the ad

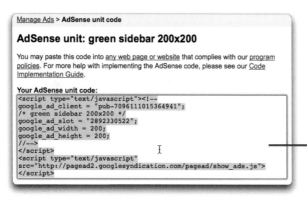

Once you've gone through the whole process of creating an ad, the AdSense site will show you the code you need to place the ad.

18 Select it all and copy it.

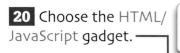

19 On the Layout | Page Elements page, click Add a Gadget.

20 Choose the HTML/ JavaScript gadget.

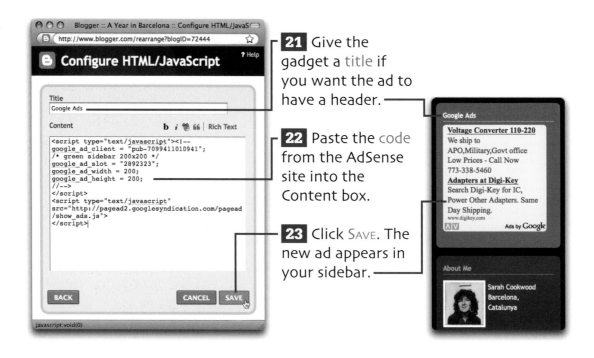

21 Give the gadget a title if you want the ad to have a header.

22 Paste the code from the AdSense site into the Content box.

23 Click SAVE. The new ad appears in your sidebar.

getting paid to blog

track your earnings

1 Once you've set up AdSense, clicking the Monetize tab will bring you to your Earnings report.

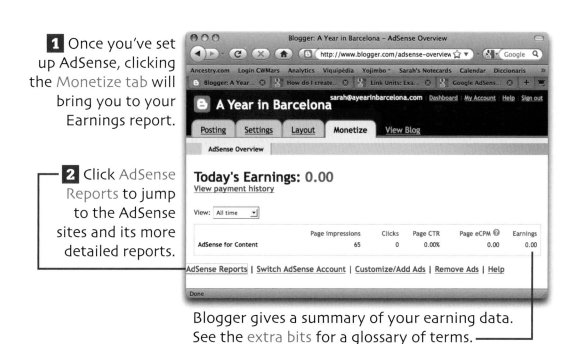

2 Click AdSense Reports to jump to the AdSense sites and its more detailed reports.

Blogger gives a summary of your earning data. See the extra bits for a glossary of terms.

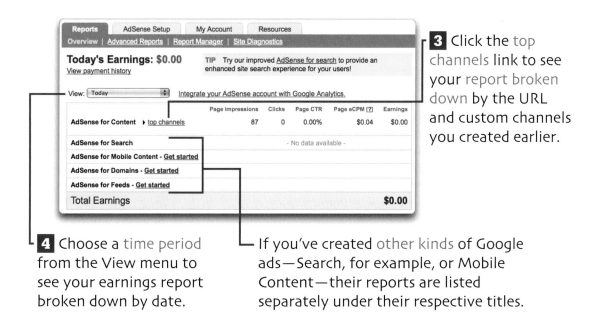

3 Click the top channels link to see your report broken down by the URL and custom channels you created earlier.

4 Choose a time period from the View menu to see your earnings report broken down by date.

If you've created other kinds of Google ads—Search, for example, or Mobile Content—their reports are listed separately under their respective titles.

other affiliate programs

1 There are many organizations more than willing to place ads on your site. Once you find one that you like, and that you think your visitors will find useful, use their tools to generate the necessary code. (This is Amazon's affiliate program.)

2 Go to Layout | Page Elements and click Add a Gadget.

3 Choose the HTML/JavaScript gadget from the list that appears.

4 Paste the ad code into the gadget's Content box.

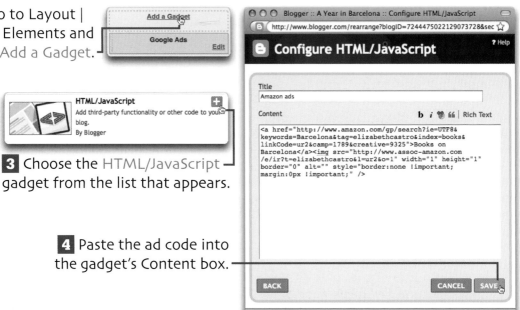

Google Ads and ads from other affiliate programs, like Amazon, can coexist peacefully and even legally on your blog.

extra bits

set up AdSense p. 153

- While you can use Blogger's automated features to add Google ads to your site, I think advertising is delicate enough to require a more careful, hands-on approach, as I describe in the next few pages.

- Just for the record, if you choose the first option on that page, Blogger will set up an AdSense gadget (see page 154) at the top of your sidebar and turn on inline ads (see page 156). If you choose the second option, you'll only get the sidebar gadget. And if you choose the third option, you'll only get the inline ads.

- Whether you use the AdSense gadget or the AdSense web site, you only need to create one user account.

add an AdSense gadget p. 154

- No matter how many AdSense gadgets you add to your layout, the maximum number of ads that will appear on any given page of your blog is 3.

- In addition to three ad units per page, you can also have 3 link units (see page 158) and 2 search boxes. Nevertheless, placing too many advertisements can annoy and desensitize your visitors and thus be counterproductive.

- If you've just set up AdSense, it sometimes takes some time for the real Google ads to appear. Public Service Announcements may appear in place of ads for a day or so.

- AdSense gadgets are either content or link units. Content can be all text, or a combination of images and text, while link units are just, well, links, but come in groups of five.

- Unfortunately, the AdSense gadget doesn't let you add a header to your ad section. You can use the AdSense web site and an HTML/JavaScript gadget to add an ad with a header, as described later in this chapter.

ad units vs. link units p. 158

- I think I find the difference between ad units and link units confusing because of the use of the word "ad": To me, they're all ad units! It's just that the link units are made up of single-line, text-only links, whereas the ad units can be a combination of text and graphics, and even when they're text-only they have titles and descriptions. (In the AdSense gadget, the ad units are more descriptively called Content units.)

extra bits

- I've only shown a small sampling of the different kinds of ad and link units available. You can see the whole collection at https://www.google.com/adsense/adformats.

format and colors p. 159

- Once you've chosen a good set of colors for the ads on a particular blog, click the Save as new palette link next to Colors so that you can use the same palette (by choosing it from the pop-up menu) for other ads.

- Unfortunately, color palettes that you save on the AdSense site do not (yet) appear in the AdSense gadget in Blogger.

track your earnings p. 163

- Channel comes from the same Latin word that gives us "canal", which offers a much more graphic depiction of ads flowing to your visitors via a particular conduit.

- CTR stands for Click Through Ratio, or the proportion of people who see the ad to the proportion who click on it.

- The eCPM column (effective Clicks per thousand) attempts to give you an idea of how well your different campaigns and ads are doing with respect to each other. Google gets this number by dividing your earnings by the number of page impressions, multiplied by 1000.

name your ad p. 161

- Unfortunately, you can't (yet) choose a named ad from the AdSense gadget within Blogger.

place the ad p. 162

- I'll admit to a personal bias against ads. The more the ad seems to try to trick me into clicking, the more they make me doubt the authenticity, content, and motives of a blogger's posts. So, I like to label the Google ads on my blog to make it clear that these are ads, that there is no subterfuge going on, and that my posts can still be trusted.

a. using your own domain

In previous versions of Blogger, if you wanted to use your own domain name, something like www.yoursite.com, you had to have your own web host and had to set up Blogger using FTP.

Blogger now lets you continue to take advantage of Blogspot's free hosting while using your own custom domain name for a professional look.

choose a custom domain

1 It looks great to have your blog at a custom domain, like www.ayearinbarcelona.com. To start, go to Settings | Publishing and click the Custom Domain link.

2 If you don't already have a domain, you can easily buy one from Google and you're all set.

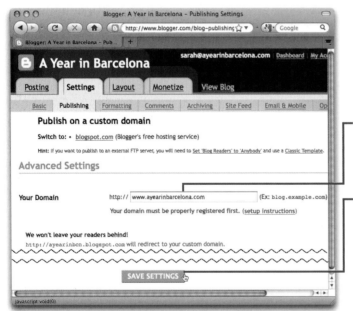

3 If you do already have a domain, click Switch to advanced settings.

4 Then type your domain name in the Your Domain box.

5 Click SAVE SETTINGS and continue on the next page.

using your own domain

tell your registrar

1 Log in to your domain registrar, and find the area where you control the DNS settings. (Not all registrars let you do this yourself.)

2 Begin by lowering the TTL (Time to Live) value, so that the changes are updated more quickly.

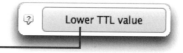
Lower TTL value

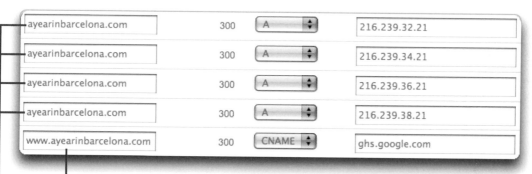

ayearinbarcelona.com	300	A	216.239.32.21
ayearinbarcelona.com	300	A	216.239.34.21
ayearinbarcelona.com	300	A	216.239.36.21
ayearinbarcelona.com	300	A	216.239.38.21
www.ayearinbarcelona.com	300	CNAME	ghs.google.com

3 Next, create one CNAME record that points www.yourblog.com to ghs.google.com.

4 Finally, create four A name records that map your 'naked' domain (for example, yourblog.com without www) to the following IP addresses: 216.239.32.21, 216.239.34.21, 216.239.36.21, 216.239.38.21.

Once you save the changes, and they propagate throughout the system, typing your domain name will bring up your blog.

extra bits

choose a custom domain

- Blogger will save your Blogspot address (for example, ayearinbcn.blogspot.com) for you so that no one else uses it. In addition, it'll forward visitors who type that old address to your new domain name.

tell your registrar p. 169

- If you can't find where to change the DNS settings, ask your registrar if it can make the change to the CNAME and A records for you.

- You can find more information on changing the CNAME records at http://bit.ly/BloggerDomain.

- It's probably a good idea to change the TTL value back to normal a few hours after you make the changes.

- It can take up to a few hours or even days for the new DNS settings to propagate, or spread, throughout the web.

using your own domain

index

A

About Me gadget 96–97
  tips 108
address of blog. See URLs
Adobe Photoshop Elements xiv
ads
  add title 162
  adjust placement 155
  ad units vs. link units 158
  affiliate programs 164
  channels 160
  customize 157–163
  design 154
  format and colors 159
  HTML/JavaScript gadget 164
  inline 156
  name (for tracking) 161
  place customized 162
  track earnings 163
AdSense gadget 154. See
  also Google AdSense
  adjust placement 155
  tips 165
affiliate programs 164
aligning
  images 38–39, 49
  paragraphs 22
Amazon affiliate program 164
announcing new posts 135, 140
anonymity
  allowing for commenters 114
  and profiles 95
archive blog 6, 15, 73
astrological signs, in profile 104
Atom format 149
Audacity, audio software 46
audio
  add to post 46–47
  in profile 103
authors. See blog authors

B

backlinks
  create 122
  display 58, 121
  hide 58
back up templates 82
birthday, in profile 104
blockquotes 22
Blog address (URL) 4
blog authors
  add 123
  list 125
  new 124
  permissions 126
  remove privileges 127
Blogger. See also BlogSpot
  account 3
  and Google 2, 3
  and Picasa Web Albums 43
  description vii
  help site xv
  icon 8
  in draft xiii
  listing your blog with 134
  new features xii, xiii
  sign in and out 10, 124
  start with 2
  status page xv
  Terms of Service 3
  user name and password 3
  Web site 2
Blogger in draft xiii
Blogger Play 134, 148
Blog List gadget 74
Blog Posts area 58–59
BlogPress 94
blogs
  about vii
  add author 123
  add new post 14–15
  address 4, 7, 11
  archive 6, 15, 73
  backlinks 58, 121, 122
  changing ownership 131

  colors in 66
  comments 112–119
  delete 11
  description 55, 70–71
  edit posts 16–17
  first post 6
  formatting posts 22, 70–71
  header image 56–57
  hide 100
  list 100
  listing with Blogger 134
  list of in Dashboard 8
  lists of 74, 134
  mobile 86–91
  multiple 12
  name 4
  personalize 51–74, 75–84
  private 128
  publicize 133–150
  publish drafts 21
  save draft 20
  signature 3
  start 1–12
  syndicate 136–138
  templates for 5, 75–84
  title 4, 57, 70–71, 78
  traffic 146–147
  useful tools xiv–xvi
  view 7
  writing 13–32
BlogSend Address 135
Blogs of Note 134, 148
BlogSpot 3, 170
BlogThis! 92–93, 122
  tips 94
bold formatting 22
books, favorite, adding
  to profile 105
bounce rate 147
browsers xiv
bylines 30
  date and time in 72
  display/hide 58
  preview 59

index

C

Cascading Style Sheet language.
   See CSS
categorizing posts 26.
   See also labels
channels
   create 160
   description 166
   tracking earnings by 163
city/town, adding to profile 104
clouds of labels 66–67
CNAME record 169
colors
   change 66–67
   of ads 166
   of title 78
   tools 22
   variables for 80, 81
commas, and searchable bits 105
comments 28, 112–119.
   See also Reactions button
   add 112–113
   allow again 130
   control 28
   delete 118, 130
   display/hide 58
   format 58
   hide 120
   leave 112–113
   link to in byline 112
   moderate 116, 129
   notification 117
   registered visitors 112
   stop 119
   subscribe to 113
   view 112–113
comment spam. See spam
Compose bar 22–23, 32
computer requirements 2
CSS 79
   adding 32
   book about xvi
   in template 76, 79, 84
CTR (click through ratio) 166
custom domains 167–170
   buying 168
   choosing 168
   DNS settings 169
CuteFTP 46

D

Dashboard 8
   and team blogs 125
   Reading List 134
   trouble viewing 30
   view profiles through 98
date
   change 27
   display/hide 58
   format 58, 72
deleting
   blogs 11
   comments 113, 118
   images 42
   links 19
   posts 29
description of blog
   add 55
   formatting 70–71
description of blogger 97
Display Name 3, 101, 109
   and profiles 98
   in About Me gadget 96
DNS settings, for
   custom domain 169
   tips 170
draft
   publish 21
   save as 20
draft version of Blogger xiii

E

eCPM (effective clicks per
   thousand) 166.
   See also Google AdSense
Edit HTML mode 32
   and moving images 48
editing posts 16–17
   shortcut to 58
email
   blogging 90–91, 94
   comments through 117
   let visitors 141
   new posts 135
   share posts via 140
email address
   display/hide 100
   for announcing posts 135
   set 101

Email Post links 59, 141
entries, blog. See posts
envelope. See Email Post links
extra bits
   description xi
   for adding multimedia 48–50
   for blogging from afar 94
   for choosing a custom
      domain 170
   for getting others to
      contribute 129–132
   for getting paid to
      blog 165–166
   for getting the word
      out 148–150
   for personalizing your blog 74
   for starting your blog 11–12
   for telling others about
      yourself 108–110
   for working with
      templates 83–84
   for writing your blog 30–32

F

Facebook, share posts via 140, 149
Feedburner 149
Fetch 46
Firefox (browser)
   advantages of xiv
   and removing images 49
   and resizing images 41, 49
Flickr
   and Slideshow gadget 64
   and URL of images 48
followers 138, 149
Followers gadget 74, 138, 149
following other blogs 139
font family tool 22
Fonts and Colors tab 68–71
   adding to 84
fonts, setting 70–71
formatting. See also templates
   Blog Posts area 58
   colors 66–67
   entire blog 51–74
   fonts 70–71
   individual posts 22–23
   remove 22
   resources for xvi
FTP programs 46

G

gadgets. See also page elements
  About Me 96–97, 108
  add 61
  AdSense 154, 165
  Blog List 74
  Followers 74, 138, 149
  HTML/JavaScript 145, 162, 164
  Labels 66–67
  layout in blog 53
  Link List 62–63
  non-Google 74
  remove 60
  reorder 54
  Slideshow 64–65
  Subscription Links 137
garbage can, for deleting
  comments 113, 118
gender, in profile 104
getting help with Blogger xv
getting indexed 142
getting paid to blog 151–166
getting the word out 133–150
Gmail, and Google accounts 11
Google
  account 2, 3, 11, 43, 114
  adding web page to 142
  and Blogger vii, 2, 3
  DNS settings for custom
    domain 169
  getting indexed by 142, 149
  Webmaster Tools 150
Google AdSense 151–166. See
  also AdSense gadget
  ads between posts 59, 156
  channels 160
  description 152
  for Domains 157
  for Feeds 157
  for Mobile Content 157
  for Search 157
  set up 153
  site 157–163
  tips 165–166
  tracking earnings 163
Google Analytics 143–147
  analyzing traffic 146–147
  set up 143–145
  tips 150

Google Groups 148
  creating 135
Google Reader 136, 139, 140

H

hash sign, and permalinks 30
header images
  add 56–57
  adjust for new template 78
help with Blogger xv
hiding comments 120
highlight color tool 22
home page, adding to profile 104
how this book works x–xi
HTML
  adding in Compose mode 32
  edit template's 79
  for links 31
  format posts with 22
  for moving images 48
  reference xvi
HTML/JavaScript gadget
  for AdSense ads 162
  for affiliate program ads 164
  for tracking visitors 145
HTML, XHTML, and CSS, 6th
  Edition: Visual QuickStart
  Guide xvi

I

image editors xiv
images 34–43
  add 34–35, 36
  add to blog via email 91
  add to blog via MMS 88–89
  header 56–57
  in profile 102
  move 37
  permission for 48
  place 36
  remove 42
  resize 40–41
  shrink header 56
  Slideshow gadget 64–65
  tool for adding 22
  upload 34–35
  view on Picasa 43
  wrap text around 38–39

IM Username, adding
  to profile 104
indexed, getting 142, 149
Insert Image tool 22, 34
interests, adding to profile 105
Internet Explorer, and
  BlogThis! 92
invitation to team blog 124
  canceling 131
iPhone, blogging with 86–91
  with BlogPress 94
italics, formatting 22

J

jump break
  adding 24–25
  edit text for 59
  tool 22

L

labels
  adding 26
  cloud display 67
  display/hide 58
  Labels gadget 66–67
  list of 66–67
layout settings 52.
  See also gadgets, templates,
  page elements
Link List gadget 62–63
links
  adding 18–19
  backlinks 58, 121, 122
  for audio 47
  from labels 67
  link units in AdSense 158
  lists of 62–63
  subscription 137, 149
  testing 19
  tool 22
listing your blog with Blogger 134
lists
  of blogs 74
  of labels 66–67
  of links 62–63
  tool 22
location, in profile 104

index

M

mailing lists, for announcing
   posts 148
Media Player 50
messaging. See SMS, MMS
Minima template 5
MMS blogging 88–89
mobile blogging 86–91
Monetize tab 153
   tracking earnings 163
monetizing blog 151–166
movies. See videos
movies and music, favorite, adding
   to profile 105
moving images 37
   with HTML 48

N

name, in profile 101
naming your blog 4
new features xii, xiii
   post editor 12
   uploading images 48
Next Blog 134, 148
Nickname. See Display Name

O

OpenID 112, 114
operating system requirements 2
others, blogging with 111–132

P

page elements. See also gadgets
   and templates 83
   description 53
   reorder 54
paragraph alignment 22
password, for Blogger 3, 12
   recovering 12
permalink 30
   definition 18
permissions, for blog
   authors 123, 126
personalizing your blog 51–74,
   75–84

phones, blogging with 86–91
Photobucket 64
photos. See images
Picasa Web Albums 43, 48
   and Slideshow gadget 64
   upcoming integration 49
Posted by option 58
post editor, new 9
   and links 19
   and Picasa 49
Post Options 27, 28
post pages 30, 112
   description 30
   disabling 31
posts
   add from toolbar 92–93
   add new 14–15
   announce new 135
   audio in 46–47
   categorize 26
   date/time of 27, 31
   delete 29
   edit 16–17, 21
   email 90–91
   email new 135
   format 22–23
   images 34–43
   labels 26
   let visitors email 141
   links in 18–19
   MMS 88–89
   number displayed 59
   preview 6
   publish drafts 21
   publish first 6
   remove temporarily 31
   save as draft 20, 31
   save automatically 15
     and published posts 30
   share 140
   SMS 86–87
   summary 25
   title of 6, 15, 91
   unpublish 31
   videos in 44–45
   view 7
Preview, button 6
privacy
   in profile 100
   restrict access to blog 128

privileges, in team blogs 126
problems, get help for xv
profiles 95–110
   audio 103
   birthday 104
   description 97
   edit 99–104
   favorite movies, music, and
     books 105
   gender 104
   general info 104
   home page URL 104
   identity settings 101
   IM Username 104
   industry info 105
   interests 105
   location 97, 104
   occupation info 105
   overview 99
   photo 102
   privacy settings 100
   search 106–107
   searchable bits 105
   share 97
   user stats 98
   view 98
   work 104
publicizing your blog 133–150
   announcing new posts 135
   getting indexed by Google 142
   letting visitors email posts 141
   listing blog on Blogger 134
   share posts via Twitter,
     Facebook, Google Reader 140
   syndicating your blog 136–137
publishing
   drafts 21
   posts 14–15
   summary 25
   your first post 6
Publish Post, button 6

Q

Quick Editing icon,
   display/hide 58
QuickTime 50

R

Reactions option 58
read more. See jump break
redo button 22
registered visitors, and comments
   112
Remember me box, when signing
   in 12
removing
   images 42, 49
   links 19
requirements 2
resizing images 40–41
responsibility, in team blogs 126
restrict access 128
Rounders 3 template 76
RSS feed 136, 148
   links 137

S

saving
   as draft 20
   automatically 15
searchable bits of profile 105
search engines, adding blog to 142
sharing posts 140
sharing responsibility for team
   blogs 126
Show Email Post links?, menu 141
signature. See Display Name
signing in to/out of Blogger 10
   on public computer 12
size of images 40–41
size tool 22
Slideshow gadget 64–65
SMS blogging 86–87
   tips 94
sound. See audio
spam, avoiding 115, 116, 117
status page for Blogger xv
stopping further comments 119
strikethrough, formatting 22
style sheet. See CSS, templates
Subscription Links gadget 137
summary, publish only 25
syndicating blogs 136

T

team blogs
   and Dashboard 125
   canceling invitation to join 131
   changing ownership 131
   privileges 126
telling others about
   yourself 95–110
templates 75–84.
   See also CSS, formatting
   adjust 78
   and header images 56, 78
   and sections in sidebar 76
   back up 82
   change colors of 68–69, 78
   change fonts in 70–71
   changes lost 83
   description 5, 79
   edit 79
   finding additional 83
   page elements 53, 54
   pick new 76–77
   samples 77
   tags 84
   tips 83
   variables 80, 81
Terms of Service, Blogger's 3
text wrap 38–39
time
   change 27
   display/hide 58
   format 58, 72
   time zone 72
timestamps 30, 72
time zone, set 72
title
   adjust color of 78
   formatting 70–71
   of ads 162
   of blog 4
   of blog posts 6, 17, 91
toolbar, blogging from 92–93
tools for publishing a blog xiv
tracking
   earnings from ads 163
   visitors 143–147, 150
traffic, analyzing 146–147
   with Feedburner 149
TTL value 169, 170
Twitter, share posts via 140, 149

U

undo button 22
uploading images 34–35
URLs
   adding to Google 142
   in Link List 62–63
   in links 19
   of audio files 47
   of Flickr images 48
   of images 48
user name in Blogger 3
user stats, in profile 98

V

variables (in templates)
   add 80
   tips 84
   use 81
videos 44–45
View Blog, link 7
visitors, tracking 143–147, 150

W

Webmaster Tools 150
web site for this book xii
Who Can Comment?, menu 114
Winer, Dave 148
wishlist, in profile 104
word verification, for
   comments 113, 115
wrapping text around
   images 38–39
writing your blog 13–32
   from afar 85–94
   from toolbar 92–93

X

XHTML. See also HTML
   book about xvi
XML. See syndicating your blog

Y

YouTube videos 44–45